Coaching Questions

101 Coaching Questions for the Coach and the Coaching Client for an Empowering Coaching Session

by Randy Wayne

Table of Contents

INTRODUCTION

Hello and thank you for taking the time to check out this book!

For many of us, the concept of coaching and life coaching might be something we are not used to. All too often, there are times when we as people assume that we understand how something works, when in truth it is not always that way. However, the element of coaching can help you understand what you need to know about this, and over time, you will be able to really get what you need with this, and sometimes, it makes a coaching session that much better.

With many people, they often want to find the answers themselves, but in truth, it can be hard. With coaching, for many people, they do need that other person, or sometimes they just need to be pushed into the right direction. Coaching will allow you to do just that, and so much more as well.

In this book, you will learn all about the nuances of coaching. This means that you will learn not only what coaching is about, but also some of the various facets and different elements of this, and how you as well can be a better coach. There are even questions for a coach or client to ask themselves, and you will learn why you ask that, and even the best possible answers for that sort of thing. Give yourself the coaching that you deserve, and you will be able to definitely and for sure have an all-around good coaching session. We will go over types of coaching as well, because there are different elements to coaching that can be a bit different for you, and this can be seen in many different ways. On the other hand, with coaching, you will be able to take whatever issues you have at hand and work on them. This book will guide you in the right direction, and by the end of this, you will know exactly how to be the best coach you can be, and the best client to a coach as well.

CHAPTER 1: What is coaching

Now, your first question might be what coaching is. Coaching is an exact form of betterment, and often, people do not realize just what it can pertain to. This chapter however, will go over just what coaching is, and how it can relate to your life.

Now, coaching is basically like what it is, it is someone that you have that is working with another person to help the other person's goal. For example, think of coaches in sports teams. Many times, you have that person who is on the side cheering you on, telling you how to do the action without royally screwing everything up. That in essence, is coaching. In truth, it can be something that people can get into to help them, and it is definitely a way to improve the relationships between two people.

Sometimes this is done in a very formal setting, where you actually go to an office, and the two of you converse there. In other cases, it is an informal setting, where there is a relationship between two people, and the two of you occasionally meet up, and in truth, it is obvious that there are both formal and informal elements to this. For some people, the coach might be someone who has more experience, or who even has expert knowledge on a subject to give advice to the other person. The client in that case would be the one receiving the advice, and using that to better a goal. In truth, coaching works o have different tasks at hand along with some objectives, along with some good development goals and general goals as well. Sometimes, you can even coach each other if the two of you are working to both overcome one sort of problem. It can be used if you have a goal that needs to be overcome, or if there is a problem you need to face.

Often, there is professional coaching that one can do. It can involve anything including improving communication skills, getting a different perspective on various elements, or even questioning or contradicting your original idea to see things from a different angle. Often, you can use this is all types of coaching, and you can use this to help overcome some sort of behavior, whether it be one that is a health problem, a personal problem, a social issue, some spiritual problem, or any sort of element. Coaching is there to help the person overcome the odds and beat it.

For some, coaching might seem like a silly thing. Some of us like to fly solo, but often, we need the help we can get from this. We might need that extra little boost, and it can be used not only to help businesses and people grow, but it can even help with mental issues such as ADHD and other much problems. Spiritual coaching can be used to help with mental issues too, and it is a means to really get you in the right sort of frame of min to look at a problem differently.

With coaching, you will be able to think critically and outside the box as well. Often, when we're going through business and personal transactions, we do not look at anything past the personal level. We only look at that, and we might look at the various elements of that too. But, let's look at it from another way, and often, big problems can be fixed in that regard. For some, it can do a whole lot of good, and in others, it can be something that can make a difference in their life in various ways.

Doing something about a problem can help a lot, and with coaching, you will be able to tackle the problem terminated, and work out a good, adequate solution to achieve the success you deserve. With coaching, you will be able to do just that, and so much more in various ways. Coaching has a lot of various elements to it that can help you, and it is something that everyone should get into.

CHAPTER 2: Why a Session Needs Specific Questions

Now, when you are coaching, sometimes you might wonder why you need specific questions. Specific questions are something that can help another person really think outside the box and work towards success in areas of life. For many people, being specific is the difference between a successful and some unsuccessful coaching. This chapter will go over what specific questions are, and what role they are striving to play in terms of where to go with this.

What are Specific Questions?

In a coaching session, you get asked various questions all of different types and mentions. For some people, it might be little questions about life and the state of it, and for others, it might be geared towards a specific action. With questions, you will be able to prompt a good response out of the client, and from there, you will have much more success.

Let's take a coaching session where you do not really ask specific questions. Maybe you just ask general ones like "what do you want to do?" or something of that nature. Yes, that is a good one once you have the problem figured out, but it is not where you should go with this. Specific questions are there to direct not only the client, but the coach as well.

If you do not tackle the specific problem at hand, you will not be successful in fixing it and bringing it back to a better state. Let's face it, a lot of us do refuse to face our problems, and many times, we just do not realize it until it is too late. Then again, with specific questions, you as a coach will be able to tackle the issue at hand, and you will be able to go over with the client exactly what is going wrong. Often, a problem with coaching is not necessarily the fact that you are coaching; it is the wrong types of questions. In a coaching session, it does make a difference whether you guide the person, or if you do not guide them. If they just go around willy-nilly, chances are, they will avoid what's really going on, and instead, they will suffer from there.

That's why you have specific questions. These questions will directly relate to what is afflicting the person at hand. This can be anything from financial issues, to even issues in their personal life such as marriage and the like. You as a coach need to direct the person's attention, allowing them to face the problem, and make the decision. These questions are used in that way, and the more specific you are, the more chances you will be able to handle the problem at hand as well.

For the Client

Now, these specific questions do not just benefit the coach, but they do the client as well. It is pretty important to see what the client can do to benefit from this, for there is a lot of elements this has to offer, and for a client, this can make quite the difference.

For starters, your client is definitely floating about, needing help and unable to do anything about it. That's what it is like. Often, if they need help figuring out a solution, chances are they've tried other things, and in general, they cannot do a damn thing about it. It sucks, but that is the way that it is with some of these people. For many of them, they might not realize just what they have to do until it is too late. But with coaching, it will take their attention and direct it accordingly.

A general question wont' help them face the problem. It just will not, and that's the truth of the matter. In this sort of situation, you need to be specific, honest, and you need to look at it from the right angles. Instead of always looking at it in a general sense, you can get specific and from there, start to work on improving your life with this in mind. With specific questions, you will be able to take exactly what you have learned and use it in a more concrete manner.

With general questions, they do work well to get the mind going. As a coach or client, they are very important to have, especially if the client and coach aren't really on good terms as of yet. But in truth, you do need to have those specific questions on hand to help you improve your life, because often, it can make a huge difference between being open about various parts of life, and not being open. When you are trying to coach, you want the client to be open and willing to speak, and often, that is done via questions that aren't always super general, but instead really nitpick at the brain, get the person to dive into their psyche, and from there, improve their life and the way that it works.

This book will go over 101 questions to help with a coaching session, and many of these will specifically get the person on the right track to help them solidify and improve the relationship they have with the subject, and along with that, you will be able to have much more success at the end of the day as well. Be smart, work on your coaching sessions and questions, and from there, you will do even better than you ever thought possible.

CHAPTER 3: Types of Coaching

With coaching, there are many different types. It is not just used for a businessperson or the like, but it can also tackle specific problems as well. This chapter will go over just what types of coaching there are, and even some tidbits about this sort of coaching, and why it might be in your best interests to try these out.

Spiritual coaching

With this sort of coaching, it can relate to Christianity in the sense that it does involve sometimes using tenets from that religion, and sometimes it can be a practitioner of that relation. Yet, it is not generally the situation, and regularly, with this type of coaching, it can be used to improve the connection one has spiritually with that of the material world.

Often, for many who practice religion and spirituality, they struggle to tap into that. That's where this coaching comes in. it swoops in so you can take the spiritual nature of yourself, or even of a heavenly body such as god, and from there, use the various elements of this to improve your lot. It is helpful, especially for those who have a bit of a religious sense to them and know for sure that this is exactly what they wanted.

Success coaching

Everyone wants success. It is obvious when people do. But sometimes, people need help working to getting success and being able to prosper, and this coaching helps with that.

With success coaching, it will go over just how to be successful in a different sort of manner, but not only that, it is also working out the kinks in life that are preventing you from being successful. Maybe there are personal blocks in the way, such as former friends who are now estranged but those words they had for you still resonate within. Whatever it may be, it is important that you make sure that you do realize there are various stops to the success of your life, and this type of coaching will work to help eliminate that sort of thing. With this sort of coaching, you can be a successful person in various fronts and manners, and you do not have to do much, besides follow the advice and work to implement it into your life. It is a good way to help work to improve your life, and give yourself the success you know you deserve.

Financial coaching

Another major problem with people is money. Money can be hard to manage, and often, people do not realize that they are bad with money until it is far too late. But often, there are means to fix this sort of problem, different sorts of actions you can take as a problem to improve your ability to handle money and be successful with it. That's where this type of coaching comes in.

Through financial coaching, you can obtain more information on how to handle money, different sorts of actions you need to take to improve your ability to be smart with money. Money is not an easy to thing to cope with, and for some people, it can be quite the struggle. But do not let it get you down, instead let finical coaching take the reins, and from there, you will be able to improve your ability to not only have money, but to manage money as well.

Typically, this sort of coaching is done by someone who is versed in the realm of money and knowing how to deal with the dealings of it. It is a resource for those who are terrible with money, which needs an extra boost to have a good sort of experience with that sort of thing.

Fitness coaching

Now, this is coaching for the body, but it is not just someone who is there behind the guy at the gym as he or she does bench presses. Rather, it is also a sort of lifestyle coaching, used to help build a better life for the person, and to help improve the effectiveness of it.

For fitness coaching, it will go over what sort of parts of the body you want to fix up. This could be anything from losing a few pounds, to even making sure that you get the right sort of foods in your body to help you tone up. This type of coaching will also give you a plan of sorts to help you reach your goal. This can also fit under sports coaching as well, and it can be used to help those who are struggling with getting better at a sport, and from there, it can help to make it easier on everyone. This type of coaching is regulated towards the body, and that's what you will be working on, but as well, it might go over the mental barriers needed to help you lose weight, and from there, you can work to have a happier, healthier body in various sorts of ways, as well as having a better life for you and your peers a well.

Law of attraction coaching

The law of attraction is something that many people do refuse to look at initially, but it is a major part of being successful. Simply put, the law of attraction is a theory where you get what you attract, and you attract whatever it is that you do get based upon what sort of person and what sort of knowledge that you have. With that being said, essentially it is you get what you deserve, and often, this is what attributes to businesses being the law of attraction does work both ways, and for those that are working to improve their business, but just cannot seem to get it right, then this type of coaching is one that can be used unsuccessfully in various elements, and it can really make a difference for many people. With the law of attraction, you go over in detail what it is that you are doing that is causing issues, and from there, you can work the kinks out and do what you like. The law of attraction is a great way to work out stops in a business if you have tried everything else, and from there, you can implement other strategies and such that will work great for you.

Relationship coaching

Now on a more personal level are relationships. Relationships can either be easy, or they can be hard to manage. Some go well, others not so much. You might have a relationship with a family member or significant others, or even in a business or peer sense. Sometimes you might have a friend that you need to work something out with. Whatever it may be, often, you need to make sure that you are being smart about the decisions you make with this relationship. For many people, relationships can be hard once you start to see the issues at hand and you are working to cope with that. Nevertheless, with relationship coaching, you will be able to tackle the problem and terminated handle it.

This can work for future commitments in terms of a relationship as well. For marriages, this does work, because sometimes there are marital issues that need to be figured out before the couple can successfully move on with their life. There are also issues such as divorces that can require some sort of assistance with it. It is something that is often required to have some sort of solace and work with, but for many, it can be quite hard. However, with relationship coaching, you can take all of the coaching and apply it to your relationship issues, and from there, you can have much more success with it as well.

Business coaching

Business coaching is a way to help get businesses on the right track. It is typically used to develop human resources and strengthen a business. It will give those in the company the support that they need, feedback on actions, and it also gives advice to both individuals and groups to give a better sort of effectiveness in the business arena. Often, it is used to help get the clients on the way towards specific goals in the professional feels. For example, if you are looking to transfer to a new career, improve your performance, help with the organization and the effectiveness, and eve improving the executive presence, this is definitely the way that it changes it. It is also used to help with those that are struggling with the comfort of the organization, and from this, it is used to build a team that works to improve the performance in the workplace and along with that, create a sort of positive impact and improve the performance. It is a way to just improve businesses to make them better for everyone.

With coaching, there are many different outlets, various reasons to help you with this sort of thing. However, you will be able to take all of this and use it to your advantage, and from there, you will be able to work to improve all facets of life. With coaching, everything does get easier, but you will need to know exactly how to do it first, and what sorts of coaching questions you will need. Do not be afraid to dive into this, and do not worry about what might happen, for it is simple, yet effective, to know exactly where you want to go with this.

CHAPTER 4: Media to Help with Coaching

Now, with coaching, there are various media that can be used to assist with the problems you might face. There are a lot of elements going around, and often, there are different sorts of issues at hand that can start to become pretty intricate over time. However, this chapter will go over the exact media necessary to improve your ability to have a better coaching session, and how to coach it adequately.

Calls

Some coaching can be as simple as calling on the phone. Talking on the phone is not only a great way to get over the fear of phone conversations, but also, to get over the nerves that seemed to become a bit stronger with those that talk. With phones, you will be able to really make it work out, and from there, you will be able to have much more success. You can speak to the person directly and ask for help with issues, and the person can give direct advice, which is pretty awesome. With phone calls, anything is possible, and you will be able to have much more success with it as well.

Phone calls are also good if you have a coach that is far away, or clients that are far away. Meeting for an hour or so each week does make a difference.

Skype

Skype is really the next step up in phone conversations, where you want to have a more direct conversation with the coach or client, but you also do not want to directly meet up, due to time or location constraints. With a skype call, you can either have a voice or a video chat, and the two of you can talk about whatever it is that is going on. From there, you can work out a plan of action, and then you can put it in. this gives a more personal connection, but does also require being around a computer or a device that docs support this sort of action.

Coffee Shop

Now, this can be a literal coffee shop, or just a direct business location where you can meet up with your partner to discuss various elements and issues. This is a good way to directly speak about whatever it is that is going on, and from there, the two of you can work out the solution. This is great if the two of you are close enough that this is possible, and it does not always have to be a coffee shop where you do meet though does determine the quality of the session at times. Sometimes, you will want to meet up in a place where it is easy to discuss various elements with, especially if the issues are sensitive. You could meet up at the person's workplace, but do not directly meet at the office. That is never a good place to discuss the sensitive matter like this, so do not bother doing that. Instead, pick correct locations that are fitting for you.

Remember that the media you use can determine the coaching session, and it is a good rule of thumb that the closer you are to each other, the better quality the coaching session, so make sure that you keep that in mind when you are determining how to do this sort of thing. The different sort of actions that you do take will determine the future of your coaching session, and it can make all the difference in a person.

CHAPTER 5: Questions for a Coach to Ask

Now that you know a bit about coaching, it is time to go over the important questions you should know. These questions are good for any coach to ask, and they can be used to help gain a better understanding of the client and the session.

    1) May I ask you a few questions?

This is used to help broaden the playing field, and it will help you get a better connection with the person.

Possible answers: sure. No.

Second question: why not?

Action: deal with getting the question answered and any sorts of tensions related to this

    2) What was great about your life this week?

This is used to help get the client to tell you about their life. This can also be used to help you get a better understanding of their situation, and get them willing to talk.

Possible answers: various answers about good or bad things

Second question: what was good about that? Tell me more.

3) Have you improved yourself this week?

This is good especially for fitness coaching, because you will be able to have them see what they've done to improve themselves and it does make a difference in people

Possible answer: various answers as to what they did improving. Sometimes they might say they didn't improve.

Second question: what did you want to do with those words? What do you want to continue to improve on?

4) What did you get done this week?

This is a good question to ask to show production in an area of life, and you can eve go into detail on if that aligns with a goal or not.

Possible answers: saying anything about what they accomplished, and the elements of it.

Second question: how does that align with the goal you have in mind. What could be done about that?

5) Do you want to be coached on this??

This is a good question that you can ask if you are given some sort of explanation on various elements a person accomplished.

Possible answers: yes/no. explanation of what.

Second question: where do you want to be coached then? How does this fit in with what you want to be coached on?

6) Did you have any struggles this week?

This can be used to assess where someone fell short, and where you should go with the next line of coaching. You can also go over what sorts of problems a person might have because of this problem.

Possible answers: whatever they feel they struggled with.

Second question: well, lets' focus on those elements. What can you do to rectify the struggle?

7) Did you feel empowered this week?

This is good especially for those with confidence issues, because often, people do not realize how much they struggle until it is too late. They start to realize where they were empowered and where they need to work on themselves, and this is good for showing them what they really need to fix.

Possible answers: yes, no I didn't.

Second question: tell me more about it.

Answers: explanation

Third question: well, how can you use this to better yourself?

8) Does your story empower or disempower you?

This is good to use if you have a client that tells you of a story of what they did, and you can show them that it might not be the best or it might be best to speak about.

Answers: yes/no

Second question: well, how can you switch the situations so that it does empower you?

> 9) Do you want to be coached on that point or did you just want to share?

Sharing is good, but you want to make sure you do not deter from the subject and make sure that it is something that the person wants coaching on

Possible answers: yes/no. I wanted to share. I felt it was relevant, etc.

Second question: well, what do you want to be coached on? How does this relate to coaching?

> 10) Are you using your experiences and problems to grow or beat yourself up?

This can be a question that could be a hard pill to swallow, because often we use our sad experiences as a pity party more than anything else. But, if you do realize that you can grow from this, it does make all the difference, and you will be able to have a much better experience in the future.

Possible answers: I am using it to grow. I am using it as a berating tool.

Second question: how can you use what happened to grow instead of being problematic?

> 11) What can you do to get a better result next time?

This is a good one to look at for those who are working to implement something into their lives. For those who are working to better themselves, this is often a tool used to see what they can do to improve it.

Possible answers: the explanation of results and talking about what they could do better. Sometimes not realizing what they could do better.

Second question: what were the problems you suffered from with this and how could you use what you learned here to make it better?

> 12) How honest have you been with this problem towards yourself and others?

Sometimes the client is not willing to be honest with them, and that can be a problem in it of itself. It is time that you start getting them on the right track, and you can do so by talking to them and getting the truth out of the person.

Possible answers: I haven't been super honest with it, I've been somewhat honest with it, I haven't been honest, or I have been honest.

Possible second question: what can you do to become more honest? What will it take to be honest about the situation?

13) Can I give an observation?

This is a very important one, and it is one you will have to be careful with. Some people love to hear observations on actions the coach sees, others, not so much. Be careful with this one in particular, because it could cause a lot more drama than you would care to have if used wrong, that's for sure.

Possible answers: sure, that's fine. No that is not okay.

Second question: alright, I will not say it/say the observation to you.

Possible answers: that makes sense/thank you for not observing.

As a note, this one is very important to get the consent of the person you are working with. For one, people often do not realize that this can be hurtful to some people, and it is not necessarily the easiest thing to get ahold of. Instead of asking right way and simply assuming, you can use this to get express consent from your client before you dive into this sort of action.

14) Is this the problem or the solution?

With many coaching sessions, sometimes people will mistake the problems for the solution, and often, it is something that does happen with time. For those that are working to figure the way around this, you should take the time to see if that is a problem, or if that is the solution. This can make a huge difference in terms of what might go down, and often, you have to look to see the problem or the solution to do something about it, so make sure that you get ahold of what it is before you continue.

Possible answers: yes this is a problem/no this is a solution.

Second question: then what is the problem/solution to this problem/solution?

15) How would you like the situation to be?

This is especially good if you are working on a problem and have no clue how to counteract this. Sometimes envisioning the situation can be the way to help improve this sort of thing. It also works well, especially for those that are working to improve their life.

Possible answers: working on building the situation, and then starting to envision how to do it.

Second question: what is the plan you need to take to get to that solution?

16) What is stopping you?

This is good for just about any sort of coaching session. For many people' look at what is stopping them, and often, this can be something that can make a big difference within many people. You have to know what the problem is, what the solution, is, and what is stopping you from getting to the solution. This can include toxic people.

Possible answers: a list of people and things that are stopping you from reaching your goals.

Second question: with those handled, how real would it be? What would you need to do to reach those goals?

17) Is there anyone bothering you?

Sometimes, the problem is not an object, but rather a person. Toxic people can be a nightmare, and for many, it can create quite the disturbance. However, if you within a coaching session start to realize the impact this is making, you will be able to see just who is causing problems, and what to do to create the solution to this.

Possible answers: The naming of people that are bothering you.

Second question: what can you do to bring a solution to this problem?

Possible answers: talking about the solutions to the problems at hand and going from there.

18) What does this mean to you?

If you are going over a plan, sometimes you say a lot, but you do not really get it. As a coach, you need to ask this so that the person has the express understanding on how this will work, and how you can use this to better yourself.

Possible answers: an explanation on the various means of what this means to them, a possible explanation.

Second question: how can you apply this?

You might have to go over this with someone a few times before they really get it, and it does help with the understanding of it all.

> 19) Are you focused on what's wrong, or what's right?

Sometimes we do not really look at the good, but only the bad. We need to make sure that we take the time to look at the good in life, and not just focus on the bad elements. In truth, this can make all the difference for some that are out there, and it does help if you are being overly judgmental about various actions.

Possible answers: various explanations on whether it is good or bad.

Second question: how can you focus more on what's right instead of wrong? What will shift your moral compass in that manner?

20) Is this the truth, or is it just hearsay?

With some clients, they might just go off of what some of the people might say, and other times, they will tell you directly what it is that is going on. You need to make sure that you do get the full story out of people, and from there, you go on and make sure that you get the full details from them.

Possible answers: this is a real thing/this was heard.

Second question: can you give me the full answers then/can you figure out the solution to the problem at hand?

21) How can you find out more information?

Sometimes, some clients do not realize that they do not know, and it is up to them to get the full details on things. With this however, you will be able to improve the mindset by making sure that you get everything squared away. You can have them search for more.

Possible answers: talk about looking for more information.

Second question: how soon can you get that information?

Possible answers: tells when they can.

Third question: what can you benefit from learning about this sort of element?

> 22) Do you want this for your own sake or is it for someone else?

Sometimes, some clients do things just for others, and sometimes for themselves. You need to get the full answer, and make sure they're not doing it because someone else said.

So

Possible answers: I'm doing this for myself. I'm doing this for others.

Second question: how can you work on that to do it for yourself?

23) Is this giving you energy or draining you of energy?

This is another important one, because it does determine whether a person is helpful or not. It also determines whether an action is good for you, or bad for you.

Possible answers: this is helping/not helping.

Second question: how could you turn the tables with this to make sure that it is giving you the help you need?

24) Is it really making a big difference in your life?

Sometimes, people believe that what they are doing makes all the difference, when it does not. You have to watch for this, and make sure that it is making a big impact.

Possible answers: it is/it is not.

Second question: how can you change this to help make a difference?

25) Do you know your limits?

Knowing your limits is very important, because sometimes people do not know that, and then they start to become slightly hung up on that sort of thing. You need to make sure you do not overdo it for your sake, and for the sake of others.

Possible answers: I do/do not. Describe it.

Second question: how can you become fully aware of your limits?

26) What do you consider your strengths>?

Knowing your strengths is essential to the success of your life, and it is insanely helpful as well. Knowing is half the battle, and it is what people will need do know to be successful in life.

Possible answer: list the strengths we have.

Second question: how can you use the strengths listed to better yourself and others?

27) What is the benefit to having this problem?

Sometimes problems have benefits, and with coaching, you have to be willing to explore all of that before making a true, big decision in life.

Possible answer: listing some of the benefits to this problem. Sometimes it might be not knowing.

Second question: well, what can this problem do to help you?

28) Will this problem help you or hurt you?

Sometimes though, some problems will hurt you instead of help. That is why you have to pick your battles and make sure that you are not doing something that will not work for you. Be smart, but also be wary.

Possible answers: the client says that it hurts/helps.

Second question: would you be better off if you dropped this problem? Why wouldn't you be?

29) What does your gut feeling say about this?

Sometimes, if you are at a loss for what to do, the surefire way to understand is to trust your gut. Doing that can make all the difference, that's for sure. It is simple, and it is effective.

Possible answers: I have a good/bad feeling about this sort of thing.

Second question: well, are you going to listen to your gut? Would you benefit from listening to what your gut has to say?

> 30) Is this problem related to something you have done before?

Sometimes connecting your problems can be something beneficial for you, and often, it can be something that will help you out. Seeing how various problems connect will do you more good than harm, because you might get to see where it would fit with everything

Possible answers: explaining how it does fit in.

Second question: what do you need to do with this current problem as it relates to the previous problem to get somewhere with it?

31) Do you have rules getting in the way of life?

Sometimes you might have some rules that you have thrown in due to family, upbringing, and the like that are getting in the way of you relieving yourself and improving your lot. You need to make sure that you do not have that just sitting in there, and you do something with it.

Possible answers: yes/no I do/do not. Sometimes listing the rules as well.

Second question: will those rules be helpful in your life if you kept them? Is it possible to do away with them?

32) How long has this been on your mind?

Knowing how long it is been on your mind does help. Sometimes, it can make all the difference and you can certainly have a much better experience with this if you do realize it is been on your mind for a while and you are working to fix it.

Possible answer: listing how long it is been on your mind.

Second question: what would you do if the problem was gone?

> 33) Is this similar to a problem you have experienced before?

Sometimes, seeing the connection to these problems and how similar it might be will make a difference in your life. You can use this to help you see the connections you are making, and it can help you really determine what it is that you are going for, along with the possible elements to keep in mind before you start to work on making sure that you have the problem taped.

Possible answer: yeah it is. Explanation of problem.

Second question: what can you do to use the information you gave me to solve this current problem?

> 34) Would you be able to change your mindset on this problem?

Sometimes you need to realize that you have got to change your minds on problems. It is important that you realize this, because it does come about sometimes.

Possible answers: I can change it/I cannot change it.

Second question: what would need to be done to change your mind on this?

35) Is this a real goal or a pipe dream?

Looking at the reality of the goal is very important. Some people do not realize this, and often, it is something that they are refusing to see for themselves. But, if you see that it is a real goal and if you realize that it might be a pipe dream in certain cases, you will be able to do something about that, and you can certainly do a lot to change it, that's for sure.

Answers: yeah it is real/yeah it might be a pipe dream.

Second question: what can you do to make this a realistic goal and not a pipe dream?

36) Does this goal coincide with your values?

You want to make sure that you are doing this for you, especially with goals at hand. Even if it is something small, you will want to make sure that you have all of that in mind and at hand, for it can make a major difference.

Possible answers: yes it does/does not coincide with my values.

Second question: how can you align the goal to let it fit with you?

37) Is this goal building you up, or is it a slog?

Sometimes you want to make sure that the goal you do have in mind is a realistic one that will work for you. You want something that inspires you, allows you to play around and make sure that you are happy, not something that is what you struggle to do with. You should make sure that the goal inspires you, not haunts you like a bad ghost.

Possible answers: it is taking a lot out of me/it helps

Second question: what can you do to not make this goal such a slog?

These coaching questions can help you as a coach inspire others, and it can be used to improve the worth of the person now, and into the future.

CHAPTER 6: Questions for a Person to Know

Now that you know of questions that can be used for a coach, these can be used personally to benefit yourself and improve what you know. This is great to help a coach think critically on all coaching sessions to improve this.

1) What did you accomplish this week?

This is good to show a coach just what they did this week, what they can use to help benefit their lives for themselves and how to improve on that.

Possible answer: the various people they helped, or maybe they didn't help.

Second question: what can you do to help more this week? How can you use what you have done to help yourself?

2) Who did you serve?

This is a good gauge for those who are looking to see who they helped this week, and also looking to assist those that are looking to understand the scope of how they helped.

Possible answers: naming various people that they helped and how it fits in.

Second question: to what extent did you help these people? How did your help benefit them?

This will help the coach really understand to what extent they are helping this person.

3) How did you grow this week as a coach?

This is a good question to ask any coach, coaching is not just something that you do with another person, but rather, it is something that you need to remember to grow in as well.

Possible answers: various situations where the coach was able to grow in different ways with their coaching.

Second question: how much of an impact did this have on you personally?

4) Is there anything you would like to improve on yourself?

As a coach, you have to learn that you need to improve too. It is not just a one-way street. You can always work on various coaching means, and from there, you can definitely make a better and bigger difference as a coach in it of yourself.

Possible answers: various information and traits that you want to improve for whatever reason.

Second question: how would improving this help in your ability as a coach? What sort of impact would this make on your clients?

5) Are you a strong enough leader for yourself and your clients?

This is good to look at, because sometimes as coaches, it can be hard to realize the impact that you make on yourself. You need to realize that over time, you will need to improve on your ability to be a leader, because a good leader will empower others.

Answer: yes/no

Second question: what can you do to improve on that?

Possible answers: various traits to work on.

Third question: what sort of plan of action can you implement to better yourself?

6) Do you feel like you are helping others?

This is a good question to pique interest with. The reason why you do this is because often, people do not realize they need to be happy when it comes to helping, which is why people need to remember that it is also based on them whether or not they are being helped.

Answers: yes/no

Second question: what can you do to further help others? What do you feel you are doing wrong in terms of assisting other people?

7) Who else will benefit?

This is a good one to ask, because sometimes people do not realize who else might benefit from this actions, and this can be a good way to get a coach to further expand themselves and give others their services.

Possible answers: my friends/family

Second question: how can you get these people to work with you and benefit from the actions you take?

8) What are you grateful for?

We take life for granted. Plain and simple. But, if you take the time to look at yourself and see what exactly you are grateful for, you will benefit from this. It is something that can certainly help others, that's for sure.

Possible answers: my family, friends, animals, etc.

Second question: how can you show better gratitude for these people?

9) Who's grateful for you?

Sometimes, we do not realize the impact that we create on others, but, with this question, you can look upon yourself and see the sort of impact you are working to improve yourself. This is a good way to help make it better for you to see just what you are doing for another person, and overall, it is a simple effective way to improve your life.

Possible answers: listing various people who are grateful for you.

Second question: how do you know they are grateful for you?

Possible answers: say why they show it.

Third question: what can you do better to improve this?

10)   Are you happy?

Being happy is something we do not really realize we're not feeling until it is too late. Sometimes we have to see that we're not creating the happiness we should be, and often, it is something that can be shocking for everyone.

Possible answers: yes/no I'm happy/not happy.

Second question: what is causing you unhappiness?

Possible answers: people/situations.

Third question: what can you do to take control of the situation?

11)   Are you honest with yourself?

Being honest with yourself is something that many coaches do not realize they forget to do. You have to be honest to really be successful. Sometimes, if you are lying to yourself, it comes off obviously in a coaching session, and from there, it can become a major problem.

Possible answers: yes/no I'm being honest/not honest.

Second question: what is preventing you from being honest to yourself?

Possible answers; people/places that are preventing honesty.

Third question: how can you prevent this from becoming a problem?

12)   Do you believe your coaching works?

You have to know and feel that your coaching works to make sure that you are doing the right thing. It is understandable when it seems you are not doing well with your coaching, and thereby do take some time and effort to make sure that you work on that as well. If your coaching works, you will work, and over time, it does make a difference.

Possible answers: yes/no I do/do not.

Second question: what is stopping you from feeling like you can make this work?

13)   Do you have a goal with every client?

Having a goal with your clients will keep you inspired to do better, and often, it can be something that will really help you. You want to have goals, because it will allow you to fulfill them over time and give yourself and others the life they deserve.

Answer: yes/no I have that.

Second question: what kinds of goals can you set up with your clients to ensure that you have one?

14)   Will your choices with the clients bring you forward or not?

You have to make sure that the choices you make with them benefit not only them, but you as well. Making the correct decisions does play a major role in improving the coaching between a client and his coach.

Possible answers: yes it does. No it is not as much

Second question? What can you do to improve that and bring you forward along with them?

15)   Will the advice you give bring better benefits to others

You want to make sure that you are using this to help benefit others. If you feel that it is not helping them, then you need to look at yourself and strive to change just that. You need to make sure you are giving those help and advice, not problems and such.

Possible answers: it is helping them. It is not helping them.

Second question: what can you do to bring better benefits to others?

16)   How does that solution help a client?

You want to make sure that the solutions you present to them will help your client in multiple ways. Figuring out the best means to help your client and the solutions you give will in turn allow you to have a much better, healthier mans to improving the life that you are working to have with others.

Possible answers: it helps in various ways. Say how it does.

Second question: what can you do to further help a client with this solution?

17) Is there any advice you would wish to get out of your system before you spread it to other clients?

Knowing what works and what does not work, and having the decency not to spread it to other clients, is a major part of coaching. For those that are working to coach, the best thing to do is to make sure that you give only good advice, because these people do rely on you, and they want the benefits listed.

Possible answers: various sort of beliefs that you have.

Second question: what can you do to get rid of them? Can you get rid of them now?

You should work with this in mind and start to work on getting rid of the possible bad things that might be lurking about.

18)   What's the worst that can happen with that advice?

You might have some advice that you are trying to determine if it is good or bad for the client. This is important, because often, people think the advice is awful, but they do need to look at whether or not a person can benefit from this, and what you can do to improve this sort of thing.

Possible answers: list out the problems with it.

Second question: based off that, is the advice worth it to use, or not to use?

19)   Is there a downside to the dreams you have

You might have a dream as a coach to get your client somewhere, but you also need to make sure that it works for you. Being smart and knowing whether or not some advice will work or not work is essential, and it is very important.

Possible answers: list the downsides to his, if any.

Second question: is there a way to continue with the pathway while limiting the downsides of this?

20) What is stopping you from giving advice to that client?

Sometimes there are a few things that are stopping you from really giving the best advice that you can to the client. You might have your own personal dislikes, or whatever you so choose. You should make sure that you know what is stopping you, and what exactly is going rough your mind, to rally see what you can do to benefit this.

Possible answers: talk about what is stopping you.

Second question: what sort of actions can you do to prevent the stops from getting in the way?

21) Who wouldn't like it if you did the right thing?

Some people out there hate the concept of people being smart and logical. They hate when people are doing the right thing and benefitting, and especially as coaches, there is a sort of need to sometimes withhold information. However, sometimes you need to make sure that you choose the right actions, so what you believe is best, and know who would or wouldn't like it.

Possible answers: listing of various people who might or might not like it.

Second question: is there a way to avoid these sorts of people so you do not have to worry about that?

22) Do you have to sacrifice anything to help others?

As a coach, there are moments when you work hard, and you practically sacrifice it all to be successful. However, it shouldn't just be a singular effort, and you shouldn't sacrifice too much to help others. If you are stressed out, overworked, or the like, sometimes it can be caused by not really working out how to reduce the sacrifices and such. That is why you need to realize the sacrifices, and then go from there.

Possible answers: listing the sacrifices that would need to be made if that sort of action happened.

Second question: is there a way to limit the sacrifices to answer your own personal happiness?

23)   Will a new skill add to your value?

Sometimes you have to make sure that you choose the right skills. Choose skills that will add to the value, of the person, and you want to make sure that these skills the coach has for the client do add to the value. Make sure that you choose the right ones, and from there, determine what to do next.

Possible answers. It does help or does not help with it.

Second question what can I do as a coach to improve the skill in the person? What sort of skill can I substitute out to make it better for the client in question?

With coaching, you sometimes have to ask yourself the personal questions that are important about this, and you will want to ensure that you do have the right sort of question there for the person at hand. Be smart about this, make the correct decisions, and from there you will have much more success and happiness, that I'm sure of.

CHAPTER 7: Client Coaching Questions to Ask

Now that you know a little on the coaching side, let's go over what the client needs to take from this. Often, a client can get a number of benefits out of this, and for some, this can indeed make all the difference in the world. This chapter will go over 21 questions the client should ask.

1) Is this advice going to help me?

You want to make sure that this advice will help with the problem at hand. Often, some coaches who are starting out might pull you in a different direction, and sometimes, a client is bad with explaining. You should ask the coach what sort of ways this will benefit you as well.

Possible answer: the coach's response in terms of the actions you must take.

Second question: how will this help me improve my skills?

2) What can I benefit from learning this advice?

You want to make sure that as a client you are getting the best advice possible. With coaching, sometimes it is hard to explain what you really want, and with this, you will be able to make sure that you get exactly what you need, and you can benefit from this.

Possible answers: the coach explains the benefits of learning this.

Second question/plan: take it all into consideration and then start to plan accordingly.

3) Do you feel I need to hone my skills?

Sometimes, you might need to ask the coach if it is necessary to hone your personal skills. You can make sure that you have a good relationship with the coach by finding out what sort of skills you will want to take, the skills you believe are right, and from there, you can move forward and work on the right skills for you.

Possible answer: the coach tells you a bit about the skills.

Second question: what actions do I need to take to improve this?

4) What kind of plan of action should I be taken?

Sometimes the coach can give you a good plan of action to move forward. You can use this to help benefit not only your life, but the life of others too. This is especially important if you are running into this sort of problem, and often, it can really make a difference in your life. You should always have a plan of action before you begin.

Possible answers: the coach gives you a sort of plan.

Second question: what is the first step needed to get started with this plan?

5) How can I take my strengths and put them forward?

You want to know what your strengths are, so you can push them forward. But often, people do not know what to do about this sort of thing initially, and often, they might need help discovering their strengths and using it. You should, as a client, as your coach for help in this.

Possible answers: an explanation of the strengths at hand and then pushing them forward as well.

Second question: is there a plan to push my strengths to the forefront?

6) How do I limit my weaknesses?

Many times, the client might be knowledgeable of the weaknesses, and often, they might start to think that it is smart to look at limiting it. However, they might not know how. A good question to ask the coach is how you can limit the weaknesses of things, and what you can do to make sure that you get that fixed up.

Possible answers: an explanation of weaknesses.

Second question: what is the first step to take when it comes to limiting my weakness?

7) What sort of changes can I make with what I have?

You need to know as a client what sort of changes to make with the life that you have and everything that you have got. With this though, you can do so easily, and without too much of a hassle. A coach can often tell you exactly where you need to go with this, and it does make a big different.

Possible answers: coach explains the changes that need to be made

Second question: where do my skills line up with this?

8) How do I increase my resources?

As a client, you will need to know how to increase the resources that you have, and often, it is something that you will have to face with time. You do want to make sure that you have a good idea of the resources you have got, because it does make a big difference in your life.

Possible answers: assessing all resources and figuring out an answer.

Second question: where do I begin with increasing the value of my resources?

9) Am I just following a pipe dream or is this realistic?

As a client, you have to control the reality of your dream as well. With a coach, you might sometimes get the answer that it is a pipe dream, and from there you will need to increase the plan of action and go for what needs to be fixed up. With this question, you will be able to ask your coach in a realistic way if you are on the right track, of if it is really intelligent to follow through with this sort of thing. When you do get the answer to that, do not fret, but instead realize that often, we might be following dreams that aren't necessarily the smartest to face.

10)	What sort of advice can you give me on (insert problem here)?

As a client, you might think you have it relatively figured out, but the coach is another person, a guy with different experiences, and it can be almost essential to ask the other person for help from time to time. By asking your client if you can get advice from them, you can then move forward, using the advice that you do have to make sure that you are going the right way, moving against the right pathway. Doing this will help you, and over time, it will make a big difference in your life. Try it, because in truth, this sort of advice is the type you never know what you might get, and it might make all the difference.

11) Will I be able to overcome my fears?

As a client, you might have a ton of fears, and often, it is something that is scary to think about, but over time, you will start to realize that it is possible to overcome the fears that you have. Fear is a matter of lie itself, and over time, you will start to realize that you will indeed get there over time. Overcoming fears are something that you will need to make sure that you get ahold of, and you will want to feel the urge to overcome them. A coach will improve the life that you are living, and you should make sure that you are smart about how this goes, and over time, you will achieve great success.

12)   How can I improve on this situation to give it value

A coach has kind of a bird's eye view on the situation at hand, and it can be remarkably helpful. By looking at the situation and improving on it so that you can be valuable, you will be able to see the truth everything. With this, you will start to see it all, and over time, it will create quite the impact, and in turn, it will vastly improve your lot, and your worth as well. By asking your coach how to improve this and create a valuable asset out of this, you will have much more success, and in turn much more happiness.

13)   Am I acting on logic of impulse

Sometimes, a client does not realize how they are acting until it is too late. If you realize that you are indeed acting out of impulse instead of acting out of logical, you will be able to see the difference in it. As a client, the coach will be able to guide you in the right direction, and if they say you are indeed acting out of impulse versus logic, you should ask how to prevent this, how you as a client can improve on this sort of action now, and into the future. A coach is there to lead you on the right pathway, and over time, this can be used to help you stay in your lane and get yourself fully on the right pathway to success.

14)   How do I go about talking to empower and help others?

You shouldn't be just getting help from the coach in empowering, but you should use it to empower others. With coaching, a client should always learn to empower other people. By asking your coach how they do it, getting the full understanding of what I is that they do, and understanding it, you will be able to achieve great success, better understanding, and much more fun in life. Remember, as a coach, they are working to build you up, so it is only fair that you work to empower other people as well.

15)   How do I increase my courage to change my life?

A scary thing about being a client is the fact that you might change. Sometimes, you might worry about changing your life for the better, but you do want to figure out how to increase the courage that you need to do this. Yes, this does take courage and yes, you are going to need to be brave. But true bravery is realizing that this indeed does exist, and you need to be realistic as well that the smart thing to do is to make sure that you do the right thing. Do make sure that the courage you have does increase, and over time, you will have much more success.

16)   What sort of schedule should I have on this?

For a client, the best thing to know is the layout of their day and the schedule which will work. Taking on this big of an endeavor is quite adventurous, and over time, it surely does become something that you need to face. However, if you figure out a schedule and formulate it to success, you will be able to improve the way things are. Over time, it'll get better, you just need to make sure that you do have the right mindset with this. Having an adequate and smart schedule is the way to success, and you should consult the coach to ensure you do the right thing.

17)   Is this really a need or value for myself?

With advice, you want to make sure that it is valuable. While a coach might think it is, and they might tell you something about it, you need to make sure that it works for you. Over time it will become obvious that you do need to watch for the correct sort of reasons that you do make sure to do this sort of thing. You want to make sure that value is there, and it is placed on the coaching session. With this as well, you will be able to have much more success and happiness, and you will do so without any sorts of failure or problems.

18)   Have you faced a problem like this before?

A coach might have the experience needed to face this problem. Shocking, right? It shouldn't be. Coaches are people like you and me, and you want to make sure that it is smart to talk about this problem and you have a good grip on this. Talking to the coach and asking for their advice and input on this is something that many people struggle with, because often, coaches might seem like these big, scary guys that you do not talk to about these sorts of thing. But being smart, making sure that you can trust them, can give you the information you need to face the problems you have.

19)   What sort of experience would I need to overcome this problem?

You would need to make sure that you have the right sort of experiences on hand to improve this sort of thing. With coaching, you do want to make sure that you get a coach who can tell you of the experiences and skills that you will need to generate success with this. A common problem with some people who go into coaching, is they believe that talking to the coach about such experience is wrong in some sort of fashion. But it is not always that way, and you will want to make sure you are comfortable as well with the experiences that you have. Get experience to overcome the problem, and from there, you will feel much better and be better off.

20)   What's the impact I'll create with this?

You will want to know the impact you can create with this, because often, it does determine what sort of reaction you will get out of this. Knowing the impact of your actions and what this will create is essential to success, and over time, it does improve the effects of this. Knowing what the future will hold will allow you to formulate a plan of action to truly benefit from this, and you will feel so much better over time as a result of these endeavors.

21)   How can I accomplish more with less of the effort put forward?

Accomplishing more with not as much effort and becoming efficient is the name of the game with this. As a client, you will want to ensure that you do take into consideration what you are going through, and you will want to improve the nature of this. You will want to ask your coach about how to become more efficient. They can lead you in the right direction, improve your success, and in general create happiness. Doing this does make a difference, and it will continue to do so no matter what.

With coaching, you have to get the client's perspective as well, and you will want to make sure that you do so before you continue. The client should be open to asking questions, and from there it can determine what should be done next, the actions needed to be taken, and the next step to achieve the success of or both parties.

CHAPTER 8: Questions for the Client to Ask Themselves

Now that we have gone over what clients should ask coaches, now it is time to go over what a client should ask himself or herself. This is important, because it makes a difference, and with these 20 questions, you will know exactly what you should ask before things get out of hand.

1) What am I pretending not to know?

Sometimes, some clients will leave their life in a state of not-knowing. They might start to pretend that they do not know the answer to the solution, but that certainly is not the case. Instead of deluding yourself and pretending that you do not know anything, start to work on improving yourself by seeing that there is some things you do know, but you are pretending not to know. Knowing this, you will have a much better experience in your life, and one that is much better for you as well.

2) Am I acting out of the faith I have, or fear?

Sometimes, some of us do act and react to situations out of fear. You have to know this, and often, it can be scary to see. You should know the difference between the two of them, and over time, it does become easier as you ask yourself that. Do make sure that you work with yourself, see the difference in that, and work towards fixing that up. Often, making sure you know the difference between the two can make all the difference in the future of your life and what you are trying to make it become.

3) If I wasn't scared, what would I do?

Sometimes, the reason why we do not act the way we went to is out of sheer fear. It is obvious when it happens, and in truth, it is hard to face. But you have to realize that the only thing to fear is fear itself, and often, if we aren't scared of something, we will accomplish it. As a client, you need to realize that the reason why you are not reaching for the stars is the fear of the unknown. Once you see that, you can start to plan your life accordingly, and through this, have much more success as well.

4) How do I increase my sureness in myself?

Increasing the sureness in yourself is something that you will have to do. You will want to look at yourself, see what you are doing to either improve or not improve your lot, and from there, start to look at how sure you are. You need to question how you can be sure in yourself, because often, the reason why people aren't confident is because of how unsure they are. By making sure that you are sure of things, you will be able to increase the success you are working towards, and you will feel way more confident in your decisions.

5) Am I confident in my decisions?

Also with that, is confidence in your decisions? Have you ever decided on something, and then you immediately regretted it? Yeah, that's something that can often come about as a result of not being confident in your life choices. However, if you start to question whether you are, it brings you forward, and this is something you will need to ask yourself. It could present another problem you can work with the coach to solve, or it will just simply bring to light all of the problems at hand. If you are confident, you can do whatever it is that you need to do, and from there, you will have much more success as well.

6) If my life was around my values how would it be like?

Sometimes visioning this and seeing what it would be like can make a huge impact on yourself. Seeing the extent that it does take and the way your life would change can help you see which values are good, and which ones aren't so good. However, you can also get the rude awakening that you do seem to get at times, which might show that you do not have the best values. This is really one of the best exercises to see your place and the values you have, and over time, you can work to improve that, make it much better, and in general, improve everything in some way, shape or form.

7) If I could take one step to make a difference, what would it be?

Sometimes seeing how you can make an impact with just one step can change things. With life, the little things do go a long way, but we take them for granted. We certainly do, and it is something we are not willing to admit to ourselves until its too late. But taking the time to pick up the little seeds we've planted, seeing them for what they are, and doing something about it, can change the game in general. Instead of just holding onto the idea that you cannot change things, start to look upon yourself and see exactly how to do it. Do not be afraid of what the others might say, but instead, work to make the impact you know you can.

8) What will I accomplish today to make a difference?

This is a way to really look at the life you have to offer, and from there, start to determine what you can do to make an impact in the world. This is a great thing to ask yourself when you wake up first thing in the morning and are planning your day. Working to at least accomplish something every single day can make a huge difference, and over time, it will certainly improve your understanding of things as well. You owe it to yourself to do this, and it will help you on many different fronts.

9) Will this advice help or hinder me?

As a client, you might get advice from those outside of the circle of where you get advice from, and you might start to question it. This is a good piece of advice for those sorts of clients who hear a lot of hearsay from their friends and peers, and they do not know what to do with it. This is especially good if you are getting advice from a source that you are not sure whether is good or bad. Look at the advice, see it for what it is, and then determine over time if it is a good thing to have or a bad thing, and you will from there be able to do with this information what you feel is best.

10)   How do I meet the needs that I have?

Sometimes, looking to see that you have needs and working to meet them can make a difference in the way you function. You should look at the needs you possess every so often, and from there, start to work on trying to improve your need for them. Sometimes, these needs will pop out at you. Other times, they will show themselves suddenly. Keep track of your needs, and from there work on trying to put it together. This is something you can ask yourselves or your coach the next time you are in a session, and they can help accordingly to steer you in the right direction and give you what you need as well.

11) What is the emotional cost of this decision?

When you are making a decision, this is in general the thing you ask yourself. With emotions, there is a cost involved. It is not a monetary cost, but in some cases it might as well be. Certain decisions have a significant emotional impact on you. You might feel good about it, you might feel bad, but you will need to remember that certain types of decisions will make an impact on you physically and emotionally, so be chary when making decisions. You should always go for the ones that create a good impact on you and your body, but also look for the decision that will not cause you so much emotional turmoil that you will not be able to function. This is an important question, and it should be asked before every major decision is made in a client's life.

12)   Am I procrastinating on this decision?

Procrastination is not the key to success. It is not, and often, it can be detrimental in certain factors. Procrastination can cause you to make foolhardy decisions, so it is not the best thing in the world to do. As a client, you must ask yourself if you are procrastinating, and why you are. The answers there can open you up to new problems and such that you might want to go over with the coach. This is a great question to ask if you are worried about where you should go next, and if you are freaking over a decision. Do not procrastinate, but instead do something about this to help yourself, and to help others.

13)   What am I delaying my actions?

You should also look at what you are delaying with the actions that you take. Some people subconsciously do delay personal actions because of their desire to make sure that they aren't offending people or hurting some sort of future decision. Do not hold yourself back from making correct decisions, and instead, try to look at if you are delaying the inevitable. Sometimes, if you do look at that, you will start to realize that you are delaying something, and you will see it for what it is, and then work to handle it. As you may already know in many cases, the client will refuse to jump and make plunges without their coach around, and that can create a giant impact in the future. But do not be afraid of it; instead realize what it is, and then go from there.

14)   How can I learn from this problem?

As a client, you will need to learn from your mistakes. See for yourself that you have problems, and instead of trying to avoid them, face them. If you do not face them, and instead work to avoid them, you will not get anywhere. Chances are, that's probably how you got into the situation that you are in. Instead of holding back though and not learning about this, you should instead take the problem, harness it, and from there, work on improving the solution over time. It is important to know that, and you will definitely benefit from learning about where your problems go and the impact that they have in life, that is for sure. Take the time to learn, and you will certainly improve the problems and the state of them over time with that and that alone.

15)   How can I enjoy learning how to solve problems?

Problems are not always things you enjoy solving. Often, you might not know how to really effectively do this sort of thing. Learning how to solve them and enjoying how to solve them will improve the way you feel about problems. Often, the reason why people hate problems it is not because problems exist, it is the fact that they have to solve them. But what if you learned how to. Maybe you can answer that for yourself, and then work on a plan to understand how to enjoy the concept of solving problems. Learning to love them is not something weird to do, but if you think about it with the fact that learning to love problems is a good thing, you will start to see the impact problems have. It is a known fact that if you do not let a problem affect you, chances are you will have a better control over the situation, and much more success to boot.

16)   Is there any benefit I know of to solving these problems?

Some might not realize the benefit to solving problems. Solving problems can be your best friend though. Often, when you are against solving problems, chances are you might start to feel the problems collapse in on you and make things harder on yourself as well. However, there is quite a benefit to solving the various problems you suffer from. The fewer problems you have, the happier you will be, because often, if you take control and solve the issues at hand, you will be able to move further with this and take on new and bigger problems. That is the benefit of resolving them, and it is why people take them in. if you are working to improve yourself, the best thing for you to do is to start looking at how to solve these problems, and you will start to see the benefits come up like a flash over time, making things even better for you as well.

17)   Am I working to take action of working on blind hope?

Blind hope is something that people start to push themselves into, and often, it is a big problem for some. Blind hope is how many get in trouble, and it is how clients start to falter. Often, working with blind hope is not a smart manner, and you might be lying to yourself. You need to take action, and not just rely on hope.

This can be a hard question to swallow for many people, and often, it is not easy to face. However, if you start to see that blind hope is something possible, you will be able to improve this over time, and you will stop relying on this. Stop decisions that rely on blind hope, and start to use logic to create a better, more successful situation.

18)   What am I responsible?

Responsibility is something that everyone needs to face. Sometimes, a client might not realize just how much they're responsible for, and often, that can lead to a boatload of problems. Many times, the reason why people claim that they're not doing something or working on a sector of the company, is because they're not responsible. But, if you do not take responsibility, you will not be able to be successful with that area, and it can make a difference between happiness and success, and stress and displeasure in a person. Realize that your success lies in your responsibility and the ability to take on certain factors, and start to work on that to improve your life business, or the like. Doing that can make a difference, and doing so can help you in multiple ways.

19)   How can I increase the zone of my responsibility?

Increasing your responsibility is something that you are going to have to do. If you are looking for increasing this, you will start to see for yourself that you are in charge of certain elements as well. By making sure that you know what you are in charge of, you can take control of it.

Maybe though, after you have controlled that, you want to see how much more of this you can control. That's where the zone of responsibility comes in. You need to know what it is, where you need to be, and all the elements of it. Once you know that, you can increase, and it'll make your life all the more easier.

20)   Am I working on this logically, or with my heart?

Finally, with decisions in coaching yourself, you have to look to see if you are following your head, or your heart. Your heart might tell you some gut instincts, but your head is where the correct decisions come in. do not make bad decisions, and instead, start to work with yourself. If you do start to think logically, understanding the situations and all of that, you will notice when you are working toward improving yourself, or if you are just working on blind faith. Making sure that you follow your head with serious plans of action instead of your heart is imperative, and often, it can make all the difference with you in the future.

With coaching, it is a personal situation that you will need to take on as well. Often, working to improve yourself and taking a personal look at who you are can make everything all the better. In truth, it can be scary to have all of that, but over time, it can be something that you will start to see over time. by doing this, you will notice that it is only going to get better from here, and it can make your life so much better, easier, and more fulfilling for you as well. So do take the time to coach yourself, for it can be the best decision that you have made, because you are looking inward to yourself and seeing everything that would need to be changed over time.

CONCLUSION

Thank you again for taking the time to check out this book!

I hope you learned a lot about coaching. Coaching is a great tool to be used in really just about any situation. There are tons of uses for this, and in truth, it can be one of the best things you can do for yourself. With coaching, you will be able to take control of the situation, and over time, you will be able to do what you feel is best for the situation, and you will be able to increase the ability and drive to become better at this as well.

With that being said, it is time to talk about the next step to take. There are really two next steps for you as well, and there are two options to go. The first, is for coaches. Your next step is to take the material in the coaching section and begin to use this to help better others. It is simple, effective, and very much helpful as well. You will be able to assist your clients with reaching their goals and dreams and you can do so without too much trouble as well.

For those that are clients reading this book, your next step is to take the questions in the client section, and either start to ask your coach about them, or ask yourself. You owe it to yourself to have success, and with these questions, you will be able to have that and so much more, easily and without too much of a hassle. Do it, and you will be reaching for the stars and achieving success in no time.

Leadership Coaching

101 Strategies for the Coach and the Coaching Client to Becoming a True Leader

by Randy Wayne

2

Table of Contents

INTRODUCTION: The Surprising Truth About Leadership

"If your actions inspire others to dream more, learn more, do more and become more, you are a leader."

John Quincy Adams

A Peculiar Story of Failed Leadership

Here is a story of failed leadership. The mid-19th century was an exhilarating time in America, most of the country was experiencing unprecedented growth, cities were drawing strong waves of rural workers, new technologies such as the steam engine, the telegraph, and the internal combustion engine. Tens of thousands of eager and industrious immigrants were streaming into urban areas that were becoming strongholds of manufacturing productivity. Historians have noted that despite a decided lack of institutions, organizations, and corporate traditions, the young capitalist country took advantage of its rich collection of resources to bring out the best new ideas from bright and inventive minds.

However, there was a dark side to much of this economic production. The US was still transitioning out of a slave-based economy that stubbornly refused to shed the moral bankruptcy of the human-chattel ownership, burgeoning city centers were ill-equipped to absorb the great migrations of Irish, German, Polish, and other European groups. But most importantly, rampant human exploitation became the norm even as brilliant inventions were developed to actually improve the human condition. In the midst of all this chaos and great possibility, a person of genius, vision, and leadership could make and indelible mark on the future of the country.

In 1866, a young man named Tom arrived from Michigan to Louisville, Kentucky to begin work as telegraph operator for the respected communications company, Western Union. He was a bright and curious kid, barely 19 years of age, but had, through a series of twists and turns landed a respectable job despite several early harbingers of a less than fortunate life.

As a young boy, he was raised by a family of modest means living in the port city of Milan, Ohio. He was always known as a rambunctious and active child that could not, and would not sit still---a true terror to his teachers. He constantly and relentlessly asked questions, some of them bordering on impertinence, and he possessed an insatiable inquisitiveness. Tom made few friends---a fact that was exacerbated by the fact the boy was born with an unusually broad forehead. The effect of having a larger than average head size combined with the constant questioning he asked of the adults around him eventually exhausted their patience.

Only his mother recognized that her little boy was not being disrespectful nor willful, but rather, he was extraordinary bright, and more than likely a bit bored from the tedium of schooling imparted on so many youths at that time. She saw his potential and proceeded to develop her on curriculum to channel his passions and voracious curiosity. In effect, she was his coach--- guiding him, giving him feedback on his studies, correcting him, and helping him harness his abilities and encouraged his curiosity.

Her decision to provide Tom with as structured and rigorous a home-school education as she could, rather than giving up on him, played a critical role in developing his sense of perseverance and fierce independence—two qualities that served him well when the first of two remarkable events that would change the course of his life forever occurred.

Two Twists of Fate and One Giant Mistake

First, when Tom was 14, he was riding a train when he noticed that a young boy of 3 had wandered unattended onto the path of an oncoming boxcar. Before he could think of it, the teenager scooped the bewildered child up and rolled away from certain injury or death. Within moments, the boys frantic father rushed forward and gratefully embraced his little boy. In a gesture of profound thankfulness, the man revealed that he was no just another passenger, but was the station agent for that train depot and insisted that the young Tom be trained by himself personally to become a telegraph operator.

This vocation was a significant educational advancement, but more importantly, being a telegraph operator meant being on the cusp of 19th century innovation. During the next few years, Tom quickly mastered not only the fundamentals of the telegraph system but specifically requested to work during the late shift so that he could perform his own personal experiments with the leftover equipment in peace and quiet. His fascination with this so-called burgeoning "communication science" became the center-point in his life as he transferred to work in different cities from the South into the Northeast. Despite his valuable expertise, Tom's initial projects regarding his various inventions met with limited success. He was often under-employed, poor, and constantly on the road to look for new work and capital opportunities to fund his rapidly refined, technologically advanced projects.

Having reached his middle 20s in dire straits, Tom set forth for New York, living little better than a street beggar until the second of extraordinary twists of fate befell him. For quite a number of days, Tom had found a way to sleep in the basement of one of the many buildings situated in New York's awe-inspiring financial district. Having emerged in a stupor one morning, and just after begging for a cup of tea from a kindly street vendor, he noticed there was ruckus on the street. It turned out that the manager of that buildings brokerage firm was in a state of panic over a stock-ticker machine in the building that had stopped working, refusing to print out quotes. For any brokerage firm, this was an all-out disaster as it effectively halted all trading. Tom quickly offered his services and within a short period of time, not only quickly diagnosed the broken gear within the system but rigged it to work again.

It is this eerie repeat of the event nearly 10 years ago, when he first saved the little boy, that Tom was rewarded richly for his quick thinking and nimbleness. He averted disaster, and the manager of the brokerage firm promptly offered him a position to repair all defective machines in the building. This arrival of a steady and well-paying job offered the required stability and financial capital that gave Thomas Alva Edison the pathway to build precisely the inventions he wanted.

Within a few short years, and before he turned 30, Edison would develop a world-class laboratory and move his operations to New Jersey, where he would work for the rest of his life, introducing the world a series of ingenious, and now indispensable inventions:

the phonograph, dozens of original designs and improvements on the telegraph, culminating in the telephone, and of course—the electric light. His works were so marvelous in design and execution that crowds of people would flock to witness his various scientific demonstrations in slack-jawed admiration. Over time, this ability to create seemingly magical results from the cutting edge of scientific discovery paved the way for Edison to be given the strikingly fitting nickname, "The Wizard of Menlo Park." But how can Thomas A. Edison, one of the greatest inventors of the 19th and 20th centuries, also be known as a failed leader?

Edison was not quite 40 years old when he meets Nikola Tesla, a 6 foot 4-inch Serbian immigrant who arrived with a formal European education and a nearly unknown reputation. But what the young engineering genius possessed was a letter of introduction from Edison's business colleagues, Charles Batchelor. In that letter he noted that, "I know two great men, and you are one of them. The other is this young man!"

At this midway point in his life (Edison would live to over 80 years), the older inventor was much revered as a living legend. He could have stopped his work entirely, never producing another invention or filed one more patent, and still be considered one of the most successful entrepreneurs of the 19th century. Yet it is at this critical juncture that Edison makes a disastrous misstep.

Looking Tesla up and down, Edison immediately recognized the natural brilliance of the awkward and gangly immigrant-inventor in front of him, but he was highly contemptuous of Tesla's development of an alternating current (AC) system. He didn't see that the more versatile AC system was far superior in conduction, safety, and reliability than the direct current (DC) model. Edison fought fiercely for direct current, which he harnessed to illuminate New York City in 1882. Having made his fame, fortune, and reputation on DC, Edison stubbornly believed that there could never be any discernable improvement on what he already established.

Soon, the venerable older genius fought a vicious multi-year war of attrition to crush Tesla's campaign to move toward the AC system. Not only did Edison fail to recognize that the majority of major urban areas that had at first adopted electrical grids were already rapidly outgrowing his original power systems, he actively launched attacks to take down Tesla, who by then, had left his mentor (who had refused to pay him for his work), to work with George Westinghouse, a visionary entrepreneur who saw the great potential of Tesla's AC model---a technology that we use today to power small lights as well as large industrial machines across great distances.

Today, Edison remains an American icon, but with his stubborn preoccupation with discrediting Tesla and his outright rejection of what was clearly the superior advancement, he never went on to summon up his previous levels of remarkably original innovation. In the second half of his life, Edison spent his time filing patents that were improvements on items he already established, or minor products. He refused to listen to colleagues and business partners. After declining to embrace the new era of AC, the famously persistent inventor poured all of his hopes and resources into another ill-advised scheme to use magnetic technology to derive iron from ore; a time-wasting catastrophe that nearly closed down his laboratory imperiled the careers of his research staff that worked for him.

Toward the end of his life, his biggest investors, such as JP Morgan, who had championed him throughout much of his career, realized the limitations of Edison's remarkable stubbornness. When Edison was able to channel his relentless doggedness toward difficult but ingenious projects, the inventor could literally illuminate a dark world and bring astonishment and delight to the masses. But it is Edison's failure to be open-minded and flexible, his refusal in exercising humility, ultimately lead to a total and complete lapse in much needed leadership.

Tesla, on the other hand, reportedly loved giving his imagination free reign rather than let it rigidly define the world around him. By his own account, his inventions existed whole and complete in his mind before he physically created them in his laboratory. He truly believed in the "magic" of science.

The Essence of Leadership

What can be learned from the experience of Edison and Tesla? Both were genius inventors, both worked very hard to develop their projects, both are considered leaders and giants of scientific advancement today.

However, it is only Tesla that would go on to truly harness the power of his imagination to push past the rigid thinking traps that Edison allowed his mind to fall into. No doubt, both men had visions of great technologies but only one of them was truly visionary when it came to leadership.

This book is about developing the skills of leadership to inspire yourself and others to be their best and reach their highest personal potential. Whether you are an already established individual who has seen a great deal of leadership success already in your life, or someone who is getting back on their feet after some major setbacks in your family or career, or somewhere in-between, where you feel you are doing "fine" but want to learn new strategies to become a breakout leader in all of your personal and professional relationships.

This book focuses on the essence of leadership: the development of thinking in the highest frame of mind such that it will bring to you the success you desire and deserve.

Who should read this book?

- If you are a person who wants to know the general skills of leadership.

- If you are a coach who wants some advanced strategies for himself or herself.

- If you are a coach who is looking for strategies for his or her client on how to become better leaders.

You will learn 101 strategies and techniques to reach your creative potential whether it is for yourself or for others. This book also focusses on the model of coaching as a special form of leadership. The qualities of a world-class coach can be applied to all industries, professions, and settings. You will see how you yourself can apply the leadership principles of coaching to bring great joy and success. But before we look at the art and craft of leadership coaching, the first chapter will talk about a core theme that underscores success overall—the law of attraction.

Good luck in your journey toward manifesting all your most dearly held desires and dreams!

CHAPTER 1: Creating a Vision and the Law of Attraction

"Create the highest, grandest vision possible for your life, because you become what you believe."

Oprah Winfrey

Vince Lombardi once said that, "Success demands singleness of purpose." In those five words, Lombardi, one of football's most beloved coaches, captures the most important lesson of leadership success---in order to achieve what you want, stay ruthlessly focused on the one essential thing that makes all the difference.

There is no room for the clutter of random goals, ideas, and half-hearted devotions. Find the one thing, the big vision, and resolve to focus on that.

Think about it, have you ever had one of those days that ran on endless multi-tasking? You wake up in the morning and begin doing several things at once, like eating breakfast, getting dressed, finding your keys, packing your briefcase, filling up your kids' backpacks, and maybe even cleaning up, making your bed, and brushing your teeth! And once you get to work, the endless juggling does not stop as you rush about attending meetings, answering emails, listening in on conference calls, or physically cleaning up. By the end of the day, even if you've moved forward in whittling down your to-do list, how do you feel? Exhausted? Frustrated? Confused on what the next thing to do might be? Wondering perhaps, why you are still on this endless treadmill of ticking items off your to-do list, but never feeling that you quite accomplished enough?

This is an entirely frustrating and futile condition. Research has shown that multi-tasking is ironically, once of the most inefficient, and LEAST effective modes that a human being can experience. It may seem like you are getting a ton of stuff done, but in actuality, your brain is not simply wired in a manner that makes doing many things at once truly possible. For starters, you actually aren't doing several tasks at one time. Instead, you are performing only one task at a time---the full capacity of your cognitive capacity.

Take for example, a task that people often perform not on its own, but usually in conjunction with something else, such as talking on the phone. You are chatting away while you are listening to the television news in the background, thinking that you are performing both equally well. Meanwhile, your brain is on quite a roller coaster ride without your knowledge. The human mind is actually only attending to one thing at a time---you are either talking to your friend, or you are actively taking in the news—not both at the same time. The actual activity your brain performs is that it toggles back and forth, switching gears, so to speak as you listen to your friend talk for a few minutes, then let your eyes and ears roam toward the TV. It may seem that you are doing both at once, but basically, your attention is pulled in so many different directions that you are more accurately *task-switching rather* than multi-tasking.

Consider how inefficient this is---you are wasting valuable time switching from one task to the other. And each time your attention volleys from one thing to another, you lose precious time getting readjusted. The lesson here is clear, dive deep, stay deep, and finish that one thing. And in terms of leadership, you must have one singular vision.

In this chapter, you will be asked to perform a writing exercise that will help you clarify your singular purpose. All you need is a pen, some paper, and some quite uninterrupted time of 25 minutes. This is not a long exercise, but it does ask a lot of you---it asks that you be utterly honest with yourself. Do not skip this exercise, even if you feel like you've done some form of journaling, writing, or reflection on dreams and goals before. Performing the writing exercise is critically important because they are fundamental building blocks of leadership coaching. So, grab your pen and paper, take a seat, and you'll begin the writing in just a minute.

After your writing exercise is complete, you'll be introduced to 29 of the best strategies for successful leadership coaching. Whether you want to coach just yourself, or others, you will find that these 29 tips apply to every person, every time.

How do I Create A Leadership Vision?

Let's make something very clear, a singular vision like the one advocated by Lombardi does not mean that only ONE goal, or ONE dream, or ONE idea is all you can have on your plate at one time. Singleness of purpose can also speak to a powerful, transformative image in your minds-eye that encompasses everything at one time. In order to craft that particular vision, begin with clarifying exactly what it is you want in your life. The following writing exercise will help being your journey toward articulating what you've been dreaming about.

First, sit with your pen and paper, and imagine the following scene: you are walking along the street one day, on your lunch break. Instead of going to pick up something quick at a restaurant, or eat at your desk, you decide to take a stroll—you feel more restless than hungry, apparently. For months, you've been feeling agitated, some of the reasons are obvious, you wish you could lose some weight, other reasons you can't quite describe.

But you know that you can't keep waking up each morning, wondering why you don't feel as excited as you'd like. You feel unsure and unhappy. You don't know what you want. And, to be sure, you aren't the type of person who believes that all negative emotions are bad---there is no denying that sadness, anger, and loneliness have a role in the human condition. But you would like to find a sense of purpose for your life.

Suddenly, across the street, you see someone who looks familiar. In fact, this person looks exactly like someone you know very, very well. You rush across the street, suddenly overcome with the urge to scream in order to get their attention, and in fact you do yell, as you start to break out in a full-on run toward them, frantically waving your arms. You feel in that moment, that you absolutely must get this person's attention. At the sound of your raised voice, this eerily familiar person turns their face toward you---a face you realize that you know intimately because...it is your face.

As you come to screeching halt right in front of this person, it dawns on you in absolute wonder that this person, standing there so casually, and unsurprised by your presence, does not simply resemble you; it goes beyond the type of striking similarity that people say their doppelgangers possess---this person IS you. The two of you have the same hands, the same eye shape and color, the same slight bow to your legs, and you both have the same down to the tiny mole on the left side of your chin, right below the corner of your lip. You stand looking at each other, exactly the same except for one astonishing difference. This person is at least 20 years older than you are right in that moment. The person who is you gets right down to the point:

"I'm here to help you change your life...if you want that." You stand there, looking at yourself. Then, you notice it, this particular "you" has more wrinkles, their shoulders are slightly more stooped, and then your gaze travels up to the gray hair. You stand there in stupefied shock, so flabbergasted you can barely move.

This person smiles at you and states calmly, as if your meeting was the most natural thing in the world, "You have one minute to ask me one question about yourself. Looking at me, you can tell that I know more about how your life has turned out than you do in this moment, and I can tell you anything you want about how your life is based on how you are living now. And, I can also tell you what your life is like if you change your life. I know it all and everything as it pertains to you, what you did, what you will do, and how it all turns out—I know all the scenarios. You can ask me anything you wish."

The figure goes on to tell you that their powers are limited, that there are some boundaries to their omniscient knowledge. They tell you that they have no knowledge of things like the direction of major political events in the future, nor can they name for you any winning lottery numbers. In short, they only know certain things, and that knowledge is solely about you, well, that is, the "future you" from an all-seeing vantage point.

You are allowed to ask one question only. What do you ask your future self?

Write down that one question on a piece of paper. Take a look at your question. Here are some examples of what you might ask: "How did my plan to write and publish my novel work out for me?" or "Did I become CEO of the company after all?" or "How many children do I have in the future?"

Chances are, the subject of your question can be boiled down to a few key words in content and in the emotions they evoke. Try to find the common idea or topic behind your question. Here's an example, let's say your question is this: "Am I divorced from my spouse?" The fact that you have allotted your one and only question to this subject effectively pinpoints the main cause of your concern in this moment...your marriage. Perhaps you and your spouse are experiencing some marital troubles at this time? Have things been difficult lately? Write down all your thoughts surrounding this question and what significance that question possesses for you regarding your emotional wellbeing.

Remember to not stay trapped inside the literal meanings of the words that come to mind, as you continue exploring the question, ask yourself what are the thoughts associated with the question? You may find that what is actually weighing on your mind is not only about the state of your future marriage, but the topic of love in general, or how you desire but feel unable to attain healthy relationships. You may also find that you have been troubled with feelings of insecurity about your family overall. It is up to you to write continuously until you feel you have gotten it "all out of your system" using the one question you asked as a catalyst to explore the depths of your psyche.

The more you reflect on this singular question that you ask your future self, you will begin to see a larger picture---a picture that reflects what you truly want your ideal future to look like. Perhaps you long for marital harmony, explore what this might look like? Is it a new home that you and your spouse just purchased because you final had enough money to buy your dream home? Or do you see the two of you on a beach as much in love as ever before? This vision of how your life is being lived is entirely from your imagination. Describe it detail, and write about how this imagery makes you feel. This beautiful picture speaks to your deepest desires. This is your "singleness" of purpose.

Manifesting Your Singleness of Purpose

Now that you have thoroughly explored your one question, try to distill your image into one paragraph. In just a few sentences, try to capture exactly what you would like to see happen. In this case, you can write something like this:

"I envision that my spouse and I are sitting quietly in front of a fireplace at the end of a long day. It is unusually cold outside, so we are happy to feel safe and warm inside. The kids are upstairs after getting a chance to play all day in

the snow. Both of us was able to enjoy this vacation because I've gotten a much better job recently where I work less hours doing something I love. We talk about renovating the kitchen and plan a family reunion in the spring. I feel secure, happy, and joyful that we are together."

Once you have this paragraph written (and perhaps re-written until it feels like you have fully captured what you are wanting to experience in your life), *create one sentence* from the paragraph. This summarizing into one substantive sentence helps you to further narrow down your intention. Write your sentence in the present tense, as if you are experiencing the image right then and there. An example of making one sentence from the imaginative paragraph above may look like this:

"I am living in such harmony with my spouse and our children where we spend time together being a relaxed and loving family."

By the time you write this sentence, you'll begin to automatically see the visual images that accompany the paragraph earlier. With each time you interact with the vision, it deepens in complexity and conviction in your mind's eye.

Finally, after you've thoroughly explored your question, crafted a detailed paragraph, and then condensed your singleness of vision down to one sentence, it is now time to go one final step---decide on one word to evoke everything you are asking to receive.

One Word for All Your Vision

This is the most concentrated form of your vision. There is no more material left to condense, and you are left with the ultimate singleness of purpose. Most people may think this is an overly simplistic idea, and that such brevity would not only end up being forgotten, but useless. After all, it's just one word, what can one word accomplish?

Well, as it turns out, a lot can happen with just one word. Read each of the following words as you would an entire sentence. Say the word out loud and pause to really hear yourself say it:

Breath.

Love.

Kind.

Career.

Healthy.

Forever.

Child.

Fire.

Inspire.

How does each word make you feel? Every word has a powerful impact in the mind of the person who utters it. This one word doesn't have to mean anything to everyone, it just *has to mean something specific for you.* Reducing your vision to a well-chosen word loads it with a great deal of power. You will feel the word and its meaning in your body. In this case, the one sentence offers up several excellent choices for the one word--- and some will happen within the sentence itself, for example: "Harmony" or "Family" or even "Love." And the word could simply show up where it has not shown up before, yet somehow, the word feels appropriate and fitting when it occurred to you. This may be something like the word, "Agreement" (meaning that you and your spouse feel so easy and loving together because of your feelings of coordination).

Again, these words may feel generic---but that is only because this example is generic. Once you are free to generate your initial magical question, and then craft your one-sentence from your one descriptive paragraph, the one word may jump out at you as the right word, just for you.

With this one word, you will be able to attract the very thing you have been imagining to yourself. **The Law of Attraction** states that everything that we see in visible universe, was once just a thought in your mind. Consider the story of Nikola Tesla in chapter one. Tesla, you may recall, was in possession of a thriving imagination, he often envisioned entirely elaborate and complex systems solely in his mind before creating them, in exacting detail in his laboratory.

You, too can create wonderful things entirely from your mind, and if you are diligent about holding these images in your head, *with a steady faith in the belief that you already possess them*, it is only a matter of time before they arrive on your doorstep.

Once you realize that everything you've ever really wanted already exists in the real world, but simply needs to be taken out of your mind, then the rest is easy—just call upon your one manifestation word and it will conjure up exactly what you want in your life. This keystone to your deepest dreams doesn't negate hard work---you still have to put in the labor of dutifully working toward your goal. But the difference in having this key word lies in how magically doors will open to you, opportunities will blossom, and a sense that you are already living the magic of your fantasy in the day to day reality of your life.

How is this possible? The Law of Attraction is both elegant in its simplicity but complex in its origins. For the purposes of this book, it is sufficient to say that a variety of new thinking writers, contemporary philosophers, as well as investigators of the metaphysical theories of quantum mechanics have worked to better describe the inner workings of this inscrutable theory. The core idea is that all matter is made up of energy particles that are in constant motion, therefore, all matter is energy, but the range of frequencies fall along a vast spectrum of different attunements.

The saying that "like energy attracts like energy" refers to the tendency for matter to match their vibrations such that the matter becomes "manifest" or somehow "physical" in the world. The Law exists not merely as a theoretical maxim, but may be reliably deployed in a practical manner, such that one may look to the genesis of thought as the first step toward the cultivation of physical matter.

Therefore, if you think something, you generate a cascade of energy emanating from that thought. If that thought is one of "low energy" such as the case with negative emotions (sadness, anger, grief, fear, pensiveness, anxiety), you will attract negative emotions in kind. But if you radiated the positive energy, thoughts, and beliefs that you actually want to feel, then the likelihood that you will attract those visions into your life increases dramatically.

Now that you have been introduced to the radical metaphysical idea surrounding the law of attraction, let's put the theory into practice.

CHAPTER 2: The 29 Universal Skills of Leadership

"Leadership is the capacity to translate vision into reality."

Warren G. Bennis

What does it mean to be a leader in your life? The popular image that comes to mind is someone others consider to be "important" or "powerful" in some way that we find valuable, so that they are given a special platform to speak to and advise others. Leaders are the people who are supposed to stand charismatically at podiums, or on a large glittering stage, to deliver a rousing speech and inspirational calls to action. We think of important political or social authorities, powerful, high status individuals, and celebrities or other eminent people as leaders because they are the ones given the responsibility to command, influence, or manage others.

In reality, true leadership is not only the ability to direct a crowd's attention, but it is also characterized by taking command of a situation that needs direction or improvement. And in that case, leadership exists in a great variety of directions, whether it is being in charge of improving your life, or the life of others. Leadership is taking charge and getting things done.

You are reading this book so you can take charge of your life, achieve your goals, and create the kind of life you want. The following 29 strategies present you with the most fundamental things to know about becoming an assertive and confident leader in all aspects of your personal and professional paths.

Before we introduce them, it is important for you to write down your goals---this should be easy now that you have clarified your one true vision. To break down your vision into actionable goals follow these steps:

- State your one-word vision.

- Look over your description of this singular vision and explicitly sate 2-3 ways that you can take a leadership position in changing your current reality into your longed-for vision.

- For example, if your one-word vision is "Home" then, after consulting your paragraph descriptors, you might end up describing your goals in the following ways:

  a. "I will take charge of letting my wife know I care about her by arranging a fun date night once a week."

  b. "I will take the initiative in sending her favorite bouquet of flowers once a month."

  c. "I will take ownership of my part in the relationship and...."

- Write each of your goals in this way of positioning yourself as a leader. This will influence the way you see yourself as an empowered individual who can affect change in your life.

Here now, it is time to translate, as Warren Bennis states it so well in the quote that opens this chapter, your "vision into reality" by using leadership. The following

29 tips may be used in any combination or deployed selectively as the situation calls for it. As you start to put your action items into effect, be sure to refer to these strategies as you go along.

1. **Vision:** Whether you call upon the visions associated with your one word (as presented for your practice in the previous chapter) or make it a daily habit to simply visualize the things, people, and situations you really desire, you must continually return to these images to develop command of your life.

2. **Listen:** In order to become a true leader, be a careful listener. It is a sad fact that most people only "hear" the other person long enough so that they can take the signal of when it is their turn to speak. When you truly listen, without speaking, commenting, or monitoring your own thoughts, you would have done something that 90% of others do not do. This makes you an extraordinary outlier in a sea of mediocre human interactions.

3. **Eye Contact:** Hold your eye contact with a person for 3-5 seconds longer than you usually do, research studies have shown that intimacy and rapport is built in the non-threatening gave of another human being. Most people break eye contact to early due to social convention (women are especially pushed to cast their eyes away in a non-challenging manner), but if you soften your gaze while maintaining eye contact, people report feeling happier and more friendly with the person they are looking at.

4. **Intuition:** Listen to your first impressions, thoughts and rumblings in your gut. This does not necessarily require that you act upon those half-formed ideas or feelings, but you must take note of them. Make a deliberate effort to stop and listen to various sensations in your body and the notions that cross your mind---they provide great clues to better inform your decisions. Great leaders heed these messages, but balance their gut instincts with evidence and common sense.

5. **Compassion:** There will be many times when you feel unsympathetic or unmoved by people

who you experience as irritating or annoying. Sometimes you just can't understand why they are the way that they are. But you do not have to accept their behavior nor condone it in order to feel equanimity toward them. This is a great gift to them, that you do not judge them, but an even greater gift to yourself to be compassionate rather than unkind.

6. **Humor:** You don't have to force a joke or be a comedienne, but you can often find something hilarious, weird, or amusing simply by paying attention to the world around you. If you see something funny, share it with another person, this goes a great way toward establishing trust and rapport.

7. **Specific:** Great leaders often have larger than life personas, they are associated with flowery, grandiose speeches, and inspiring calls to action. But in reality, great leadership is the stuff of modest and specific details. That is, a competent leader will provide concrete answers to the questions of who, what, when, where, and why. These are actionable items that bring about real

progress---and isn't that the point of following a great leader?

8. **Honesty:** Honesty is an absolute non-negotiable trait for a leader. There are not varying degrees of candor, there is the truth on one hand, and the non-truth on the other. Within in the bounds of appropriate compassion, speak the truth all the time.

9. **Story:** Today's society is abundantly rich with information, statistics, and the latest scientific research, especially in service to the field of human development and self-improvement. At times, this treasure trove of useful materials can prove overwhelming in its rawest form. The development of story around the data creates a relatable narrative and reaches out to the person listening in a very human and effective way. Try to use the power of story craft to get your point across.

10. **Example:** Like the arc of telling a story (tip #9 above), or similar to tip #7 (be specific) giving examples serves two major purposes, to build a

bridge of rapport and excitement to your audience, as well as provide a concrete example of what can and should be done so that the listener is not set adrift in a sea of vague platitudes.

11. **Integrity:** Similar to tip #8 (honesty), possessing integrity is also a non-negotiable and required trait for any good coach or leader. Integrity draws on the old maxim, "do what you said you would do" where the leader follows through on stated calls to action. This uniformity in behavior demonstrates that the leader can be trusted to keep their promises.

12. **Vulnerability:** Too often mistaken for weakness, vulnerability has gotten a bad reputation for being the human quality that allows others to take advantage or exploit a person who dares to exhibit exposed defenselessness. Nothing can be further from the truth. Admitting that you have made mistakes, or have been susceptible to poor decision making in the past can be repurposed (after your lessons are learned, of course—mistakes must be processed so that you arrive at a greater level of progress, do not present

your mistakes as an educational experience if you haven't completed that assignment yet). Create a safe space for you and others to be vulnerable with one another.

13. **Innovation:** What would happen if you started a revolution? Leaders look to advance, improve upon, and re-orientate classic solutions to new problems. They also see the possibility of new solutions to old problems. Innovation requires creativity deployed in service of an already skill set, that is, get good at something, and then get creative with your skills. But most of all, innovation requires courage, so be brave and advance your novel idea!

14. **Consistency:** Unlike integrity, which is defined as keeping your word, or "doing what you said you would do," consistency is about developing a routine that will work for you to most efficiently advance your life. If you go to the gym each and every day, you will quickly find you are stronger and in better shape. Our habits make our lives, so be sure to establish healthy habits. Be consistent in your application of values and principles, as

well as in your behaviors. People pay attention to your reliability.

15. **History:** Aside from the tired cliché that those who do not heed history are bound to repeat it, there is the notion of creating and keeping legacy. Truly great leaders will look at their own history and their client's history---what has happened before? What are the major mistakes? What can be learned? What is worth keeping and preserving? Please note that these are also the questions that can help you hone in on what is your "single mindedness of purpose" when you were performing the vision exercise in the previous chapter.

16. **Plan:** There is no underestimating the power of organization. Having vision, charisma, and drive is one thing, but if you cannot remember if or when you followed-up on that networking meeting for your new career, or if you missed your daughter's science fair because you got caught up in another new project, then you will not get very far on your journey for greater success.

17. **Partner:** Great leaders cannot do everything alone. Your singular vision for the future may be your own, but there are a variety of endless tasks, not to mention challenges and obstacles, that will require that you seek out and create synergy with others. This is not only good advice here, as a strategy to increase your own leadership skills, but is necessary to frame your coaching relationship in this manner so that your client will understand the importance of this strategy.

18.   **Language:** How do you use choose your words? Do you use them carelessly without thought? Are you more precise and think before you speak? Do you curse? Do you use colloquialism? Research has shown that individuals are deeply but subtly influenced by language and word choice, and the right word at the right time can make a world of difference in how advice, guidance, and support is needed (and the converse is true---the wrong words at the wrong time may torpedo an otherwise good relationship). Here, it is wise to listen to the client

themselves and see what words, imagery, and metaphor they guide themselves toward.

19. **Resources:** Look around you, what are your resources in terms of expertise, knowledge, materials, that you have at the ready? Taking stock of what you need for your journey to a greater, more fulfilling life will help expedite your adventures. Let's say for example, that you envision learning to horseback ride because you love horses and have always wanted to learn to ride. A question about resources is more about what you need to have rather than just what you need to do. Where are the stables in your area? Who are the best instructors? What equipment do you need to purchase?

20. **Dignity:** There is nothing more inspiring than a person who is following their dreams. At the same time, there is also few things more annoying than someone who talks constantly about their self-improvement schemes. Other people are usually happy for you, but if you tend to then brag, lecture, or impart your new "wisdom" that you've acquired in your everyday

conversations, or make unwanted announcements about what you are doing next, that is not exhibiting dignity. Be a model of self-respect and restraint, so that others will be moved by your choices rather than bored or contemptuous.

21. **Excellence:** Whatever you choose to do, do it well. The reason why you have received half-hearted results in the past is likely because of your half-hearted efforts. Pursuing excellence requires a measure of thoughtfulness. What are your core values and beliefs? How do you go about implementing your values throughout your day? How do your choices reflect your beliefs and so on? Excellence is constant number of choices over time.

22. **Role Model:** Actively cultivating and getting to know role models can offer a world of benefits to your success journey. Find and pursue (respectfully, of course), the people who you wish to emulate. And do not limit yourself to traditional models of success---it is fairly easy to find an example of a successful entrepreneur, or a well-

educated person, but do not overlook the especially kind family member who is always a great listener, or the neighbor who exhibited extraordinary courage in their youth. There are many ways to be great, look for role models in all avenues of life you'd like to pursue.

23.　　**Pay it Forward:** In support of tip #22 (role model), think of yourself as being a role model for others.　Leadership　requires　deliberate mentorship, so seek out new avenues in which you can become useful to others who are often younger or less experienced than you. Likely, these up and coming individual would love the chance to better understand how they might become more like you. There are many opportunities to serve in your community, so look to church groups, worthy nonprofit organizations, and community groups. Performing mentorship to those who really need it can be one of the most rewarding experiences you can have as a leader.

24.　　**Negotiate:** Good leaders, if they are able to harness the required skills of vision (tip #1), good listening (tip #2), planning (tip #16) and tip #19 (resources), then they are well on their way to being a master negotiator. A good negotiator, contrary to popular belief, is not a ruthless, unscrupulous deal maker who operates with the sole purpose of getting as much from the other side as they. Instead, truly masterful negotiators have a profound understanding of what the other side truly wants, not so that they can exploit them, but to better give them what they want in balance to their own stated preferences.

25. **Diversity:** Variety is the spice of life. And this adage is useful for all aspects of your life. Be adventurous in your food, but also your friends, meet new people, do new things. Most importantly, learn new things. Yes, the routine of your habits provides you with an anchor for creating sustainable success (do things that bring about good results long enough, and you will receive the results you desire). However, being open to a variety of different experiences creates dynamic tension in your life which leads to greater satisfaction and happiness.

26.   **Grit:** Big corporations often spend big bucks to conduct all kinds of personality testing, however, research in the field of industrial and organizational psychology has shown that there are very few characteristics that actually predict how an employee may actually fit into the organization. But most managers do agree, those who show determination and drive to perform their jobs, even when that work is tedious, boring, or unrewarding in the short term, are the most well-liked, respected, and productive colleagues. So, to be a great leader, be persistent, persevere in spite of setbacks, that is, be gritty.

27.   **Respect:** This strategy calls for the two-way street component of respect---you must give respect to receive respect. Be a person who treats everyone (and this is everyone, form the person who serves you food at the restaurant to the CEO of your company) with the same regard and esteem.

28.   **Loyalty:** In the same manner that tip #27 above (respect) requires reciprocity (you must be loyal to others in order to receive loyalty) in order

to operate. Being loyal to yourself and to others does not mean you blindly support or condone behavior and actions you support---if you cannot defend the value of something or someone you find offensive, it is vital you step away. Loyalty, in this case requires a judicious support of those who have earned such trust and allegiance.

29.   **Reflection:** There will be many times when you will become so busy pursuing your dreams and goals that you forget what they were so prized and valued by you. Why work so hard when you have no idea why you are doing so? This strategy involves building in "pause" moments in your pursuit of excellence. Be sure to practice a form of grateful, quite reflection ideally every day. Your mind and body will thank you.

Now that you've been introduced to the most tried and true strategies for becoming a leader in your life, we will now look at strategies that help you cover the role of leadership coaching to enhance your game.

CHAPTER 3: The 18 Skills for Coaching Yourself

"I think the most important thing about coaching is that you have to have a sense of confidence about what you're doing. You have to be a salesman, and you have to get your players, particularly your leaders, to believe in what you're trying to accomplish on the basketball floor."

Phil Jackson

What exactly is coaching? To start with, we need to take a look at the very special role that coaches play in society. Most people are familiar with athletic coaches who work with athletes and sports players of all ages in order to help develop their prowess in that particular game. Coaches are the ones who run you through drills, correct your swing, monitor your improvement, and in general develop your skills in context of the sport.

But what if you consider that life itself is a sport? That there are skills and strategies that life requires of us to "win" at the game of life? If that is the case, then it goes to reason that coaching is a form of hands-on leadership. Where leaders may act as far away or removed figures, coaches have to be right there, close to you and in your space to guide you through to your goals.

Below are 18 tips for how to be your own best coach. Again, like in the previous chapter, you may modify, mix and match, or otherwise create your own coaching profile to best suit your needs.

30. **Simplify:** It really boils down to a simple matter of math. If you find yourself swimming in extra possessions, the overall effect is that you will feel weighted down. Physical objects take up space in your closet and in your head. And the care, cleaning, and storing of them will weight you down. Do yourself a favor and begin looking at your items, one by one. Can you do without that badminton set? Or that extra hope chest, or shoe rack? Do you really need 10 sets of beach towels if you don't live near the beach?

31.   **Brainstorm:** It is a shame that brainstorming as a creative, idea-generating exercise is mostly used only in corporate or organizational settings. But the technique can be used every day, and in a very practical manner. To do this, sit or stand near a place where you can write comfortably and at length. Set a timer for 10 minutes and write continuously all that is on your mind about your goal. You may find that during your writing, it turns out that things you were meaning to do are not needed, but instead, you may have an even better idea.

32.   **Movement:** Many people dread the idea of exercise, but there is good news---any movement, no matter how small, is simply better than none. That's right, you don't need to run 8 miles a day, or compete in mixed martial arts contest every weekend to reap the benefits of movement. So, go take a walk, stretch, work in the garden, touch your toes, or play a round of golf or tennis. The major benefit here is that it all counts as progress. And the remarkable result will be that once you begin raking up these small victories, you will

begin to feel like the bigger challenges are possible to overcome.

33.   **Eating:** It's no secret that what you eat has an enormous impact on the day to day quality of your health. The National Consumer Council reported that over half of American adults at any given time are currently on a diet. There is a seemingly endless array of diets and food choices you can make. Which diet is the best one? As cliché as it may sound, the best diet is the diet that works best for you. But making the conscious effort to improve your relationship with food, along with tip #32 on movement, will create the support structure to reach all of your goals.

34.   **Get Social:** One of the key ideas behind coaching is that it's the feeling of support and feedback which drives you toward excellence. In order to cultivate this for yourself, as your own coach, you'll need to reach out to others, network, make connections, and in general create for yourself a crowd of people. Getting with others means sparking ideas, getting insight, and most importantly, having fun.

35.   **Style:** You are not what you wear. But if what you are wearing is distracting to either you, or to the people around you, then it might be time for a style update! You don't have to go to great expense and purchase the latest fashion trends, because great looking style happens anywhere and can be found at all price points. Take stock of people around you who you feel speak to your aesthetic, how would you describe their look? Colorful? Playful? Pretty and polished? Rugged?

36.   **Stop Monitoring:** It might be counterintuitive, but the number one was you can successfully and quickly achieve your goals is to let go of their outcome. When you put pressure on yourself to "be happy" or to "get going" or to not think negatively, you end up thinking of that very thing. The human brain is wired to focus on the very thing that you are trying to avoid. There are values to all human emotions, and to relentlessly pursue a few, such as joy and happiness, while ignoring others, like sadness, is denying the warning signals of these emotions.

37.　　**It's all in Your Head:** Remember how annoyed you were when you were stuck in traffic the other day, which made you late for the event that you absolutely had to attend. You felt so angry that you were sweating and utterly exasperated when you arrived almost 30 minutes late. It would be easy to link the source of your irritation to the traffic delay, but when you think about it rationally, you are angry at the idea of being late. You felt negatively because it is your belief in the value of punctuality. To make this subtle shift is freeing---you should now realize that most everything you judge objectively as good or bad, can be modulated in your mind—through your approach and beliefs that you hold.

38.　　**Meditate:** It is important to find time to reflect in stillness. The ancient practice of sitting meditation (sitting still, focusing on one's breath, gently redirecting to the breath, and letting thoughts move in and out of your consciousness). This redirection toward finding stillness within ourselves is enhanced by the next tip #39 where ego is put in its place.

39.   **Take Down Ego:** Here the term "ego" is not merely a description of the part of the human experience which is arrogant, but rather the notion of one's own "false self." It is the voice inside your mind that criticizes, doubts, and is entirely judgmental of you and others. Taking down ego is challenging because the ego always tries to justify its existence. Meditation and stillness (or prayer) can help redirect the ego and quiet it down.

40.   **Vibrate High:** Recall from the previous chapter the idea that all the universe is made up of energy which vibrates and emanates forward at different frequencies. Over time similar energies are drawn together---"like attracts like" and therefore, it is imperative to exude a high, that is, positive sense of energy in order to received that from the universe.

41.   **Just Do:** One of the biggest misconceptions in the self-help industry is the notion that you must feel good all the time in order to be successful, happy, or productive. This is simply not the case. Too many people make the mistake

of believing that they must overcome their feelings of procrastination in order to become productive---but in reality, you don't need to feel any particular feeling to get started in what you are doing. You can simply start. And it is this false belief that one must feel motivated to begin, when in reality, your feelings are fleeting and may not reflect the real truth of the matter, which is that your thoughts are not who you are...but they can become things in the real world.

42.	**Be Shortsighted:** While you have now in your possession, a short list of goals that you are working toward accomplishing, once in a while, it is helpful to train your focus away from creating strict goals and objectives and instead focus on whatever you can accomplish at hand. It is similar to being a "home cook" versus being a chef. The chef may have designed dishes meticulously in their mind, and then setting about to find and put together those dishes. However, a home cook simply looks around at what he or she has available. Referring to the goal of having a happier marriage, you may have the goal of taking your spouse out to a fancy dinner every week, or you may simply decide to create a romantic outing closer to home---the end goal still gets you closer to your vision of a more satisfying relationship.

43.   **Be Insecure:** Nothing lasts forever. This is a fact. People and animals grow old and die, buildings break down, cars stop running---this is the way of the world to devolve into chaos. However, we do not accept this, the human impulse is to create extra security around ourselves---we frantically waste energy by running around making sure all the doors are locked to the point where we are scared more often than not. What if we exercised prudence (lock the door) without fear? To do so means that we have to accept the impermanence of all things. If we did this, most likely we will become free.

44.   **Be Open:** Many times, once we have our goals in hand, many people charge off in pursuit of them, without ever returning to re-evaluate them. But to be vulnerable, to be open to what the universe tells us to do, even when the signal is to give up on the goal requires a willingness to be

open to any and all messages surrounding us. If you are charging hard toward a goal, but nothing seems to be changing or working, stop for a moment to consider what this means from the standpoint of the universe.

45.   Fail Often: Our society places such a premium on success, that we rarely acknowledge failure, even though failure is truly the best teacher. Think about this, when you first learn to play an instrument, the majority of the notes you struck were wring notes. But each and every time you struck a wrong note, what happened? You stopped playing, went back to correct the note, and then moved on. You can only ever learn to play and instrument when you make the wrong notes. And if you are given permission to fail, you can learn without fear---failure, in this case, is freedom.

46.   Be Helpful: One of the best ways to coach yourself is to help others. It is extremely easy to get so involved in your own self-improvement plan that, in a strange way, your ego becomes strengthened by your own well-intentioned pursuit of success. Aside from meditation (which allows you to minimize the tyranny of your thoughts by having you see them as temporary and not who you are), the best way to get out of your own way is to volunteer to help others who are in need. So, find your local community centers and see how you too can become active. You'll find that *you will be helped* in a much deeper capacity than even the people that you helped.

47.   **Be Grateful:** In a similar vein to tip #46, you want to be able to get out of your own head (away from your ego) by realizing on a daily basis, the remarkable gifts that you are receiving on a daily basis. Beyond "counting your blessings" with the obviously amazing things in your life such as your family---but something as simple as your favorite brand of coffee, or the fact that the weather is nice. These are miniscule things that make your life better, why not appreciate them? If you are grateful for the small things, you will find the big things will be gifted to you.

48.   **Do Everything with Awareness:** This last tip for coaching yourself involves creating

awareness as you engage in each and every task. If you are writing an email, pay all your attention to that email. Honor the recipient in your mind. If you are washing dishes, think about the sensation of the water and soap, and be grateful for the meal that was on the dish right beforehand. Anything and everything can be transformed into a pure moment of reflection and bliss if you choose it to be so. And living with this kind of awareness will enhance every aspect of your life.

CHAPTER 4: Coaching Your Clients / 54 Tips on Coaching Your Clients

This last chapter is devoted to your clients. We will focus on 54 tried and true strategies for pointing your coaching clients toward taking actions that will improve their health, get their schedules organized, make time for family, excel in their careers, and create the lasting loving types of relationships they desire most. Being a leader yourself, you are well equipped to help others take the lead in their own lives.

Up until now, you have focused on strategies that are focused on enhancing your life, but when working to coach others in leadership, there are several guidelines to keep in mind. Below, you will see how these guidelines are so significant because up until now, as you have worked on coaching only yourself, that it is not always easy to take a step back and become objective about someone else's life.

But not to worry, you will see in this chapter that many of those tips for enhanced leadership that have been introduced earlier can be very easily modified to better apply them to potential clients, employees, or any others that need and would welcome your help. In order to better pivot yourself from a "me" orientation to a "them" orientation is to keep the following principles in mind:

First, get to know 3 things at the outset about your coaching client: 1) Their overall vision of what they would like their lives to be. This list should be highly descriptive of the exact kind of life they would want. 2) The most important people in their lives. And 3) What they want to immediately change about their environment.

- **The vison board**: which we introduced in chapter 1, and put to good use in chapter 2, will be a good starting point to talk to your coaching client about what they envision for your future. You should get to know their board as a window into their dreams. Is there a big, beautiful new house right in the middle of the board? Is it surrounded by lovingly tended vegetable gardens and pictures of adorable dogs? Then, you'll know that they are looking to build a loving home base and tip #41 "just do" can be suggested with regards to getting them to go to a series of open houses in neighborhoods they live in to take tours of their dream homes. Knowing what your client really, truly desires in their life can make all their difference for giving them just the right advice at the right time.

- **_The support group_**: some of the most important people in your client's life are very likely the biggest reasons why your client wants to change their lives for the better. Are they wanting to get healthy and lose weight so they can look and feel great for their spouse? Do they want more energy to play with their children? Having knowledge of who the client considers their inner circle of friends gamily directs you toward understanding the client's motivations for change, as well as additional, valuable insight on how to leverage their help. For example, in pursuit of their goal to learn to play the saxophone, you can call on your client's spouse to keep an eye on their practice week by week—your client now has a village of those who love and support them.

- ***First things first:*** What do they want to immediately change about their environment? Having your client name the most urgent stressors in their life can save you time and energy when it comes to coaching. Knowing that they absolutely hate their job is a clear signal to prioritize the vision of working at a job they absolutely love, rather than their less urgent goal of learning Spanish or planting an herb garden. It is like surveying your kitchen, taking stock of your recipes, and seeing the potential to create all these delicious dishes---none of which can taste very good, or even be made, when in fact, your stove is on fire! So, identify the things in your client's life that is "one fire" so that you can both focus your resources, and tailor your best leadership tips for these critical projects.

Now that you have some guidance on what to consider in general before plunging in to coaching your client, here are 50 strategies to apply in helping others reach their full potential. Some of these techniques are quick and easy, others are more involved, some will apply for many situations, others are much more specialized. Mix and match as you go along, relying on your intuition about what works best for different people.

49.   **Know Their Vision:** By now, you should not only be able to recite your vision for exactly what you want, but you should know theirs as well.

50.   **Know Their Strengths:** Every person has qualities that are definite assets, ask them what they think these are. Are they resilient? Do you practice great listening skills? Are they intensely creative? Assess these strengths for yourself---do you see them in the person? Rethink this list, what strengths do you perceive of them that they themselves do not see as strengths. When they meet the inevitable challenges in pursuing their goals, this list be come in handy.

51.   Know Their Weaknesses: Just as important as knowing strengths, to know their weaknesses opens a window to your client's core, so you better understand how to help them, and to perhaps using the instances when they stumble in their weaknesses as coaching moments.

52.   Remind Them it's a Process: When times get tough, tell them that "It doesn't matter where you start but where you end up." This will put mistakes and the inevitable missteps into perspective.

53.   Ask Them "What's the Worst That Can Happen?": Sometimes clients will stagnate because they have an unformed fear about a worst case scenario---challenge them on this and ask them to fully explore what would happen if the absolute "worst thing" comes to pass. This exercise helps empower them in two ways, first they can see the unlikelihood of that very thing actually happening, and two they will appreciate how quickly they are able to come up with solutions and/or face the consequences.

54. **Encourage Sleep:** Strangely enough, an effective way to help your client is to get them to sleep more. While it may be tougher to push healthy exercise and eating (clients know these things already and these changes are difficult to implement fully), gently nudging them to go to bed earlier and earlier is much easier than you think, and reaps a world of benefits.

55. **Check in Often:** Connection is key, keep in touch at least once a day via text, email, or ideally a phone call. Even a 5-minute conversation can help someone feel cared for and is encouraging.

56. **Get Personal:** Your client has a private life of course, but when it is appropriate, make sure you check in on them that there are not major family, career, or social stressors that are weighing them down. For the amount they are comfortable enough to share, get to know your client's needs this way.

57. **Less Bad News:** It's important to know what is going in the world, but with the abundance of world-wide media coverage, it is vital to encourage your client to consume this material just enough to be informed, but not to flood yourself with negative imagery every day.

58.   **More Good News:** On the flip side of tip #57---find more good news to share. Find media stories of good news and read them, send funny video clips to share.

59.   **Create Rituals:** Put aside time to pour a hot cup of tea or coffee, or take a slow walk, or read a poem. A small, purely pleasurable ritual will create a sense of ceremony and space to breath every day.

60.   **Write Your Vision by Hand:** Every day we are constantly on our phones and laptops. Rarely do we jot much down---but there is something special about writing something by hand, so encourage your client to journal, even if it is only for a few minutes, by hand each day, reflecting on or reaffirming their vision.

61.   **Go One Level Up:** As your client makes progress, it is important to keep a steady pace of improvement that hits the balancing point between being challenging but also within a reasonable reach---a "stretch reach" Ask them to describe the next concrete level they can pursue. This agreement on the doable next step will keep the momentum going.

62.   **Ask one question every day:** Challenge your client by asking one provocative question every day, such as "What is the most valuable thing you own---and what would you trade it for?"

63.   **Make One Contact:** To facilitate creating a network that supports your client's goals, ask them to reach out to one person a day that is associated with their goals. It can be someone they already know, but the idea is to move them forward on their projects by getting them to make contact.

64.   **Give A Sincere Compliment:** One, well-crafted and thoughtful compliment a day reminds them they are special.

65.   **Help Them Reframe:** When a client gets stuck on interpreting a situation in a negative way, ask them, "What else could that mean?" and wait

for 5 replies. Push them on this and they are reminded that situations have multiple meanings. Therefore, they can choose a better understanding of the situation.

66.   **A Token:** A token is a small item that you can carry around with you that has significant meaning. Ask your client to choose a small item (a pebble, a shell, a chess piece etc.) give it a meaning, and have them carry it around as a reminder of a valuable lesson.

67.   **Smile:** It works to lift your spirit every time.

68.   **Go for a Walk:** Like tip #67 this is an instant spirit lifter. Being out and about in nature will lighten your mood.

69.   **Be Playful:** Get up from your desk and twirl around, sing out loud a silly song, do something to switch up the mood---it will remind you of how silly life can be.

70.   **Be Biased Toward Action:** It is very easy to become bogged down with planning things down to the smallest details, free yourself from

this trap by always "doing" something rather than only thinking it.

71.   **Make a Game Plan:** Having stated the wisdom of tip #70...you and your client should have a plan of action. It can be something simple shared between the two of you, but it should be an organized plan of attack.

72.   **Get an App:** Smart phones are now not only ubiquitous, but have powerful software and interfaces to keep track of your goals, productivity, and connectivity with a network of likeminded others.

73.   **Power Breakfasting:** Plan out your day's objectives while eating a healthy breakfast—this creates the sense of ritual and ceremony (tip #59) as well as draws on the usefulness of a game plan (tip #71).

74.   **Meet Your Client's Significant Others:** If you really want to help someone achieve their potential, you must get to know the most important person in their life. Set up a meeting,

you'll find this contact very important for many reasons.

75. **Have Homework:** Write down one thing that will help your client achieve their goal that they can accomplish overnight.

76. **Take on One of their Goals:** Maybe if their goal is to lose 5 pounds, why not buddy up with them and do the same thing...it will give you both perspective and provides them with support.

77. **Build in a Break:** At times, when the going gets too tough, tell your client that it is okay to walk away. For those of us who are rebels at heart, or who love to question the world, it is actually beneficial to have the option that it's possible to quit, stop, or pause. When we are told "no" our souls can push back against being pushed down. Remember that you don't have to stop, just like you don't have to keep going---but simply having the option to quit is often all that is needed for you or the client to keep going.

78. **Commit Publically:** If your client is trying to achieve a goal that would benefit from crowd sourced support---suggest they promote it on social media. Without being obnoxious about it, sharing your intentions with a supportive and fun group of friends can be expand your help by several fold, and magnifies the support they receive.

79.   **Travel Somewhere:** Even if it is an overnight stay in the next city over, suggest to your client that they get out of town. This gesture of symbolically "getting out of their rut" will impart a sense of importance and ceremony around their life dreams and goals. Have them travel someplace new to reflect upon their vision as needed when the time comes for a fresher perspective.

80.   **Simplify:** This tip was reflected in the tips for high level self-coaching, but should definitely be applied to your client---have them pare down their belongings on a regular basis to things they love and enjoy. This clarifies their life as well as their goals.

81.   **Let the Mind Wander:** Some of the most creative solutions occur when you are window shopping, doodling, taking a shower, or taking a long walk. It is during routines that require very little attention that we often let down our guard. When you or your client are bogged down, or even when you've worked at length on a project, allow the mind to roam free. You may be surprised at what happens.

82.   **Making a Chain:** If productivity is part of their vision (such as writing a novel, or running a marathon), have them record their progress in a symbolic way---such as dropping coins in a vase or stringing beads on a string—the visual representation will keep them moving along.

83.   **Hand Hold on One Thing:** If you find that your client has hit a slump, ask them to name one small thing—the absolute smallest task they can accomplish that day and then ask them to do it in front of you. You can for example say, "Make that phone call now, I'll wait." This may seem like a parental gesture, but this small gesture of

concern is often enough to get people moving over a bumpy spot.

84.   **Make Them "Disappear":** Get your client to free up more time for themselves by having them say "no" to volunteering for people or projects that they do not want to do, but feel pressured to complete because of the expectations of others. Remind your client that they should only complete projects that they are currently passionate about. This permission to say no makes them less available to time and energy vampires (these include people as well as ill-advised projects).

85.   **The Stop-List:** In a similar vein to tip #84, have your client write down all the things they want to stop doing. This list should include events and projects that are no longer fun, necessary, and/or appealing. Have your client write them down, briefly describe what they are, and then have them tear up the paper. It is liberating to not be burdened by doing things that are not of value to you anymore.

86.   **Work in Cycles:** A key productivity issue is exhaustion. But you can often short circuit the system of mental fatigue by working only in increments of 25-90 minutes and taking a break (5 minutes to 30 minutes). This stop and start will allow time for rest and spacing so that you can continue working throughout the day.

87.   **Remember The Best:** Having a keystone memory will be encouraging for your client when things feel helpless or have hit a standstill. Have them tell you about a key peak moment when they felt great peace or success so that they may embody these sensations.

88.   **It is Only Now:** Remember that in whatever capacity you are working, you only have the moment that you are currently inhabiting as the key moment where anything works. The past is gone and the future is theoretical. Bring your client back to the moment if you find them lost in either looking forward or backward.

89.   **Power Snack:** It's a small thing, but have your client create a power snack that is healthy

and tasty. And then, whenever things slow down or they hit a slump, they can circle back to take a break and have their power snack...somehow it is reassuring and feels comforting.

90.   **Take on an Offbeat Creative Hobby:** If they have never ever wanted to learn to crochet, or tap dance, or raise orchids, gently challenge them to do something outside their comfort zone. Taking on a new hobby tilts their perspective, especially if that hobby has never occurred to them before.

91. **Write a Love Letter:** Have your client write a meaningful letter to someone who has been important in their life. Very few people write letters anymore, but the act of creating a grateful and meaningful letter will remind your client of their great fortune to be loved.

92.   **Treasure The Failures:** When a client hits a setback, have them write down one past failure in detail and then describe 3 things they learned from that event as well as 1 major thing

that became better because of what they learned. This will put their "failure" in perspective.

93.   **Mini Vision Board:** We've already talked about making a vision board, but making a smaller, more portable version serves as an exciting reminder of what they really want. Ideas for what they can do is to create the board online, or use a regular sized piece of typing paper instead of a big poster board.

94.   **Master the Music Game:** Make a playlist of productivity music and play it every single day. Your mind and body will become instantly attuned to begin working as soon as you hear the first notes on the first song, it will become automatic.

95.   **One Song Wonder:** In keeping with tip #94 (mastering the music game), ask your client to choose one particular song that really rocks them out---that they love it so much that it instantly gets their heart racing and their body moving. This will be their anthem. They can play

this song whenever they need to be "pumped up" before a big meeting, event, or just to get to work.

96. **Name One Person**: Sometimes, despite our best efforts, we truly falter in pursuit of our goals. A times like these, we just don't see the point of working harder, so we are willing to put off our efforts or even quit. If your client is at this crossroads, have them think about one person that would really benefit from them achieving their goal, and have them visualize that person as the recipient of these benefits. For example, if the goal is to lose weight and become healthier, ask the client to think of their spouse or child, who would gain a great deal from this goal (they have a healthier spouse or parents). Most times, we are willing to do things for people we love more so than ourselves.

97. **Be of Service**: Volunteering for a good cause gets your client involved in the city or neighborhood you live in by agreeing to help tutor an at-risk high school student, spend time with those less fortunate, are all things that bring high

value to not only the person involved, but to an entire community.

98. **Name What is Under Your Control:** Sometimes, a client will feel so overwhelmed that they do not realize that they have much more control over the situation than they do---and many times, that control begins with their own actions. Have them make a list of things they are currently able to control in that moment; it will bring clarity to a stressful situation.

99. **Name What is NOT Under Your Control:** By the same token, have them write down the list of things that they cannot control. It will also be counter-balance to the above listing of things that they are in charge of. By differentiating what you are able to control from what you are not, creates precision in your plans and objectives.

Finally, the last two tips for successful coaching involve taking the perspective that leadership coaching is a dynamic, sometimes exhausting, many times exhilarating, but always worthwhile journey that anyone can take. Make the most of your life by becoming a leader.

Always remember:

100.   **It's Another Day**: The way we handle setbacks is often more important than how many successes we accumulate. Have your client describe how they will handle a disappointing situation by drawing on strategies they have employed in the past. Also, walk with them through different scenarios where they can apply those strategies to any current disappointment. This will serve to remind them of their resilience and provide a game plan for how to effectively approach setbacks next time.

101.   **Be a Role Model:** Create a life that you love and your client will always have a model to emulate. Your life and how you lead it is the greatest and most instructive inspiration for those around you.

CONCLUSION: Putting it All Together /Creating Visionary Leadership

'I feel that a great coach is one that has a vision, sets a plan in place has the right people in place to execute that plan and then accepts the responsibility if that plan is not carried out."

Mike Singletary

Congratulations! You are well on your way to becoming a world class leader in the parts of your life that you have decided are the most important. No one can ever take away this vision of who you are at your best self.

By now, you have seen that the path to becoming a great leader or coach can happen in many different ways, in fact, a 101 pathways. But what brings all this great variety together, how do you make your choices between suggesting your client tip #73, power breakfasting (where you make your plans of the day through the morning ritual of eating a good and health breakfast), or the power tip #68, power walking (using your walking time or morning run routine to prepare for your day as well). Well, it all depends on the schedule and temperament of the client, which are both types of information that a good coach would either know already, or certainly get to know of their client. In this case, questions you should ask are:

- Is it possible my coaching client can perform both tips and modify them so that ding both can make sense and impart high value? Perhaps they can perform their power run *and* then have the power breakfast. During both times they can create and reflect on their various to-do lists, or hone in on the "one" (or 2-3) things that they must accomplish that day. If they only have time and/or energy for one of the power tips in the morning, then the next step is to ask the follow-up questions that determine what are the most important priorities in the household:

    o What are the other significant influences in the client's life that would narrow down the choice? For example, if your client has a family, especially one with small children, then the inclination is that the client will want to spend time with their children during breakfast, at which time, the power breakfast rule of planning out your day may be distracted by the joy/horror of having breakfast with a toddler—they simply can't concentrate at that time. On the other hand, maybe they have older children who may relish the opportunity to have their parent talk to them about their plans for the day. This can be a bonding experience when a mom or dad says to their kid, "Hey, I need to get this thing done today, and it takes these different steps. Which thing should I do first and why do you think this?" Your child will be so surprised that you would seek their insight and share your personal decision making that they will likely offer an interesting insight or suggestion. Try it, see if it works.

As you can see, there is no straightforward or blind application of every coaching strategy. There are no one size fits all principles. In the absence of universal rules, coaching becomes something of an art form, and you must be flexible to better serve your client.

Another important takeaway point of this book is the following: you alone get to decide. While in this book, we have talked a lot about the importance of your inner circle of family and friends. We have called them your co-coaches or your assistance coaches because they are your partners in better decision making, quite simply, you can't nor should you even try to go at it all alone. Further, you need not only their help and insight, but you need to consult them. But no matter how much your life's objectives are entwined with another person, you alone get to decide. It can be incredibly easy to forget this distinction, especially when your goal or objective is tied up seamlessly with someone else.

For example, many people reading this book, wish for a passionate, romantic, and inspiring relationship with their spouse or significant other. This may seem like a dream that involves the input of two people---and in many ways it is. You simply can't be the sole partner in a partnership. However, you will quickly realize that beyond providing this other person a loving and compassionate presence and hoping this will influence them, you cannot make someone else do anything.

You are the only person in control of your decisions, and you alone get to decide. This realization may be frightening, but it can also impart a sense of freedom--- you get to do whatever you want. So, while it is vital to beam only the most loving positive energy to those around you and the ones you cherish most in your life, know that you can only affect your desires and dreams through your own actions. Your leadership behavior is your own, so...own it!

Finally, with so many great techniques to better focus and train your mind, there is no doubt that you can feel overwhelmed, turned around, or otherwise confused by what your next steps will be, but the one final truth of being an extraordinary leaders and coach remains: it all starts with your vision.

In the day to day living of your routines, it's easy to either get caught up in unexpected chaos (a flat tire on the way to work, a suddenly sick child at home, a forgotten meeting at work), or to lose yourself in the monotony (same lunch each day, same drive home etc.). The key to staying focused in the midst of the latest mini-crisis, or to try and break out of a ho-hum and boring routine is to consult your visionary goals (tip #1). What are your objectives? What are your wildest dreams? To keep those in mind will be your anchor when all is going awry in your schedule, or your kick starter when your engine has slowed down considerably. When you go back again and again to your visions, you'll see how easy it is to choose just the right strategy, just the perfect principle, and the most terrific tip to coach yourself or someone else to a better life.

Best of luck on what will surely be a fantastic journey into joyful leadership!

www.ingramcontent.com/pod-product-compliance
Lightning Source LLC
Chambersburg PA
CBHW021427170526
45164CB00001B/131